POETRY NOW

RESPECT TOO

Edited by Andrew Head

First published in Great Britain in 1997 by
POETRY NOW
1-2 Wainman Road, Woodston,
Peterborough, PE2 7BU

HB ISBN 1 86188 459 1
SB ISBN 1 86188 454 0

FOREWORD

Although we are a nation of poetry writers we are accused of not reading poetry and not buying poetry books: after many years of listening to the incessant gripes of poetry publishers, I can only assume that the books they publish, in general, are books that most people do not want to read.

Poetry should not be obscure, introverted, and as cryptic as a crossword puzzle: it is the poet's duty to reach out and embrace the world.

The world owes the poet nothing and we should not be expected to dig and delve into a rambling discourse searching for some inner meaning.

The reason we write poetry (and almost all of us do) is because we want to communicate: an ideal; an idea; or a specific feeling. Poetry is as essential in communication, as a letter; a radio; a telephone, and the main criteria for selecting the poems in this anthology is very simple: they communicate.

Faced with hundreds of poems and a limited amount of space, the task of choosing the final poems was difficult and as editor one tries to be as detached as possible (quite often editors can become a barrier in the writer-reader exchange) acting as go between, making the connection, not censoring because of personal taste.

With this fast moving world, technology and science have found many alternatives to using animals in cruel situations.

Many people are against the unnecessary experiments and slaughter of defenceless animals for our own reasons of vanity - but still animals do not have equal rights. We still have the malicious battering of seals for fur, the slaughter of elephants for ivory, the harpooning of whales and vivisection.

This collection of poetry represents the voices and opinions of all those who are against animal cruelty. All of the poems are diverse, honest and truthful in this on-going debate.

10% of the sales from this anthology will be donated to the Respect For Animals Association and its campaign for animal rights.

Respect Too features a poem written by Spike Milligan and in buying this book, you too can make a stand and hit out against the vicious killing of animals for people's selfish want to look good.

The success of this collection, and all previous *Poetry Now* anthologies, relies on the fact that there are as many individual readers as there are writers.

CONTENTS

THE FLEA

I've got a flea
on me
But I can't find
where he be
He's not on my belly
he's not on my bum
So where has he gone
and where is he from?
I've been scratching my head
So he might be there
somewhere in my bloody hair
He doesn't sleep at night -
that's when he starts to bite
He gets into my public hair
I must get him out of there
How long will he stay?
I wish he'd go away
today.

Spike Milligan

THE LUCKY ONE?

One lovely day in mid-July
A handsome pheasant strutted by.
To find a field of corn he must
Feed away from dawn till dusk.
For when the combine harvester arrives
He must flee from man and gun.
Let's hope this time he's the *lucky one*.

Edith Briggs

CAT AMONG THE PIGEONS

Near Dysart Harbour I can
see them
collectively, respectively
tapping on the
ground floor
as Mrs Wilson strews and
scatters
in liberal - handedness
yesterday's pan loaf
cubed finely.
Ginger rests alongside;
stretches, yawns,
reclines luxuriously; this
striped, bewhiskered
herd of the flock
regards the featherbacks so
confidently and
fearlessly
turned towards him
where appropriate
'He'll no' touch them,'
she cries
and indeed with
verifiable accuracy
for surely a pigeon with
bread-stuffing
far surpasses one
without . . .

Annie Glass

CANINE CAPERS

Dear dog I hope you're going 2 behave
If we tidy up the mess mam won't rant and rave
U chewed her slippers a tasty meal
She takes U 4 walkies U won't stay at heel
When she's exhausted and comes home each night
U lick her all over till she looks a sight
Dear dog promise, when I shout you'll come back
But! Wait at the door, don't get stuck in the cat flap
Don't sit on that chair you'll get it full of hair
Leave the budgie alone and get down off that chair
Dear dog don't poo outside the yard
Mr Smith 'found' some and skidded for yards
We all love U but you're as daft as a brush
We throw U a stick but U just sit and look.
I'm off on my hols, so don't sleep on my bed
If mam catches U, it's caput or U R dead
When she leaves the Sunday roast on the sink top
Please don't eat it or you'll B 4 the 'chop'
Keep off next door's garden and leave the cat alone
Bury your treasure in our yard especially your bone
Dear dog when U read this letter please take note
If U do misbehave we will swap U 4 a goat.
Love & Chocy Drops
Irene

Irene Witte

POLAR EXPLORER

White furred explorer
largest of living bears
powerful swimmer
venturing far across the frozen wastes
hairy sole your secret weapon
against the ice pack's slippery surface
mighty beast
armed with fearsome paws
sporting sharpened, toughened claws
a nightmare vision
lumbering towards the unwary
through the mist of swirling snow
feeding upon playful seals
captured with remarkable skill
and consummate ease
visions of a cuddly creature
dissipated
emerge from the freezing water
blood soaked muzzle
fresh from the kill.

Paul Birkitt

CLUNY

Cluny boasts not only an abbey
with medieval repute
for overlap of monks standing patiently
in stalls chanting relays of offices.

A state studfarm echoes with clatter of hooves
as docked horses standing patiently
stamp in vain to scatter clouds of flies
coming back and back to attack their tailless rumps.

Derek Rawcliffe

ANIMALS' PAIN

Grievous harm to certain animals
Can cause an imbalance in other minds
With upset, anger and frustration
Showing humans darkness, with no kind

Animals were given to us for beauty
Not to let them suffer in pain
But stupidity that has grown in some
Shows grotesque thinking of people's brains

Let's realise our mistakes and change them at once
And not ruin what was given for free
Because one day we may never view
The beautiful animals that we now see.

Suzanne Heath

RESPECT FOR ANIMALS

I have respect for animals
Especially my horse
Because I like to ride it
Over a cross country course.

I have respect for animals
Especially my dog
For he keeps up with us
When we are jumping logs.

I have respect for animals
Especially my cat
Because he hunts around the stables
When we're out
To catch a rat.

Keith L Powell

THE RIGHT TO BE FREE

Soft silver skin sparkles, splashing through the sea,
Gentle, gliding movements under the ruffled sea,
A free spirit bursts through our tangled web of life,
A soft silky smile,
Full of trust and understanding,
A friend of the highest quality,
A gentle loving bottle-nose nudges you firmly,
In all the confusion and hate of our world he wants to play in his,
Turning sharply and diving like a falcon into the depths,
He squeals in anticipation of the oncoming game,
Happy wild and free,
Flipping and finning feeling his home,
Soft and warm around his body,
Filled with the joy of his freedom,
Home.

Round and round at a slow repetitive speed he swims,
Buoyant and yet unstable,
Slow decadent, flipping back and forth,
Circling , darting, disturbing, displacing,
Stillness, then,
The slow repetitive clunking of the man-made filter,
Lying motionless he slowly nudges his mate lovingly,
A low chatter emerging from his smiling face,
As he once again begins his circle of captivity,
Behind the smiles lies a low spirit,
A penned beauty waiting to burst free,
The blue walls surround his home,
He feels the soft warmth around his body of home,
But he is not,
Prison.

A Tolhurst

I RESPECT

I respect the world in which I live;
I respect my peers.
I respect the sky above me;
I respect my living years.
I respect my parents, who gave me life;
I respect those times of tears.
I respect my wife and family;
I respect all those dears.
I respect the things we all take for granted;
I respect all those fears.
I respect my experience of life;
I respect all of life's arrears.
I respect nature, for my life;
I respect death as he quietly nears.

And; I respect animals who aid in my life.
I respect animals and try to save them strife;
I respect animals who make our life bright,
I respect all living things within my short sight!
I respect animals, for the life on earth;
I respect all animals in nature's rebirth . . .
and I respect the animals, after all, they were here first!

I respect animals and especially those who are my pets,
I respect animals, well, in all respects.
I respect animals, after all they never go to war.
All our lives would be better, if we respected animals more!

Some animals will kill us, if they us. I have respect for that.
All animals keep mankind going, from whales to a tiny rat . . .
Animals respect us, shouldn't we pay that back?
Respect for animals cannot just stop at pets, your dog or your cat . . .!

Ron Matthews Jr

7

PROPHECY

Puddles, dimpled by the warmth of heav'n's haphazard tears
Grey skies crying sadly, sorrowed by our fears
Chickens fold their wings away,
Bury their heads from the weeping day.
And there, on the bank, stand the steadfast cows
Unworried by rain as they solemnly browse.
Cows who have suffered the sharp pains of birth
And licked the new life as it slipped to the earth.
A mother whose calf should fulfil all her needs
But is taken to satisfy man's cruel greed.
Before he has known the warm sun and rain
He is bundled abroad and then ruthlessly slain.
And still a cow will look at you with deep and thoughtful gaze
She does not hate the human race, their cruel and barb'rous ways.
Perhaps she feels the pity that maybe, one day we'll need.
We have set ourselves to self-destruct, a useless selfish breed.
But still the cows will be there, munching quietly their fill
On a dim and distant greenly future hill.

Penny Scales

STRAY DAYS

He keeps running
To the centre of the road
To stare at the quick creatures
That dodged his stare
And almost ended his days
Unaware that they cursed
His curious wanderings
Into the path of their mechanical ways.

Lee Ryder

OH! FOR THE VANITY OF MAN

Innocently, lies the little seal pup
Unaware of man, with the deadly club.
Cruel are the blows, pitiless is your torture.
Agonising, is the pain you must endure.
In such a savage way, you were slain
The blanket of snow, no longer clean.
Oh, for the vanity of man.

Quietly the tiger prowls, deep in the jungle
His fur coat, shimmers in the Asian sun.
Unaware is he, of the mighty hunter's gun.
Suddenly, the bullet flies from the barrel.
Mercifully, the aim was good
The needless death, sudden and quick.
Oh, for the vanity of man.

Slowly, does the giant elephant wander
On the vast and grassy plains.
Downwind, creeps the great white hunter,
Coldly shooting, till his prey falls over.
Shortly after the tusks are crudely taken
The painful suffering does finally end.
Oh, for the vanity of man.

How lovely does the ivory look?
When china would do better.
How warm is nature's coat of fur?
When imitation does not differ.
Kindly stop this global slaughter -
And respect our existing nature.

Stephanie Bones

UNTITLED

Earth was made by God
All life and souls therein
Each plant and creature for a purpose
Not for us to judge its worth

It is not for man to take the life
Of any creature that He made
To kill, in the name of sport
In mindless violence - without thought

All those hunted suffer so
The hunter's little mercy show
After long and torturous pain
Lifeless bodies cast aside with disdain

Should we not give each animal
The treatment we humans expect
And give every living thing
Humanity, dignity, above all Respect.

Elizabeth Amery

THE FUTURE?

As it leaps,
across the screen,
you see the strips,
glint orange and brown.

It captures
your imagination,
keeps your gaze fixed.
But then you realise,

It no longer exists.

Marian Lloyd

THE LABORATORY

They're crying in the night.
Endless rivers of salty tears
Not wondering why
But wondering how
Trapped behind bars
Strangling iron chain
Strung in a restraint
To have that sharp silver current
Pass through
To watch how they jump.
Continuously stuffed full
Then starved to skin and bone.
Fixed on a table
Then made to run until . . .

They're crying in the day
Only we won't see
Can't hear
Don't want to.

Naomi Cook

TESTING

Testing testing 1, 2, 3!
Look what you are doing to me.
Testing testing 3, 4, 5!
Against all odds to stay alive.
Testing testing 5, 6, 7!
Waiting to go to heaven.
Testing testing 7, 8, 9!
Half of you humans think it's fine,
When you're putting my life on the line.
Testing testing 7, 8, 9!

Sarah Howley

11

OLD ELEPHANT GREY

Elephant grey in majestic play
Size so huge
Giant steps upon the earth,
Trumpet sounds; heard miles away.

African, Indian elephant two.
An ivory train on Africa's plains.
Wise old elephant remembers you;
Don't poach again the ivory train.
Leave elephant grey; free reign.

Old steamer train cross Africa's plains
Look out from windows; elephants again.
Gigantic bull; head of train,
Trumpets on his ivory domain.

Walk, run, stampede the gun.
The ivory is theirs to stay.
Troop on, old elephant grey
Troop on. old elephant grey . . .

Patrick Humble

WILD AND FREE

I want to roam wild and free
I want all you humans to love me
But all you want is to use my skin
To keep the money you earn rolling in
You wallow in your world of wanton greed
Can't you see our sad pleading eyes of need
We don't want you humans to always show us neglect
Can any one of you out there give us a little respect.

Dawn Maureen Kingsbury

LET ME OUT!

'Let Me Out!'
calls the penguin, behind the cage.
You wouldn't like to be here,
not for any wage!
Cruelty is capturing animals that should be free;
in prison they remain, behind bars never able to see
their homeland or friends
never roam at their will;
in jail, sentenced for life,
their soul *they* kill;
simply for the pleasure
of the public domain:
and, anyone who is innocently imprisoned would also go insane,
so I take action on the penguins' cries.
I'll protest, until my eyes
slowly close and I drift off to sleep,
but at least, I wake up able to keep . . .
. . . my freedom . . .

Adele E McCafferty

BIMBO
(cat flu)

Your feline beauty soft and lief,
Have departed, hence my grief.
You who never nagged, or asked me why?
Or racked your brains for things to buy.
I saw you suffer, heard you cry,
Only once, then watched you die.
Thank you for the joy you gave,
May I grow to be as brave.

Philip Williams

A MAN'S BEST FRIEND

His master was no more around
They'd buried him in the ground
Through the wind and rain
He'd waited in vain
Enveloped in sadness profound

When the mourners had gone away
By the newly dug grave he lay
It snowed overnight
Of time he'd lost sight
He was found by searchers next day

He died where he wanted to be
Mourning love he'd known splendidly
So with tender care
They buried him there
By his master respectfully

They discussed words to be engraved
On the headstone yet to be laid
Without exemption
Drawing attention
A memory that would not fade

Here lie two souls at life's end
That all who read will comprehend
They lived as they died
Always side by side
A man and a dog his best friend.

Patricia Whittle

THE ELEPHANT

They do not understand why I like elephants.
The children mock me, giving me as presents,
Stuffed toys with beaded eyes and curled up trunks.
So now I am surrounded by these graved images:
Some made of porcelain intended to hold eggs;
Some merely ornaments;
One, huge and pink, upon a bookmark,
brought home from church, carries the legend:
Faith will move mountains.

I smile and thank them and point out
That in some cultures elephants
Are gods, like Ganesh welcoming
Diety of the doorway. Yet still
I know they think I am eccentric.

But I remember on a summer's eve
When I was ten years old, or not much more.
Bound to a wheelchair by a broken leg,
My sisters pushed me, struggling to the top
Of a steep hill which led out of the village,
Past an old pub, still called The Lugger Inn,
And to a field where a big canvas top
Had been erected - the first I'd ever seen.
Of all the many wonders that we saw
That night, most vivid still the memory
Of the small elephant, with wrinkled look,
Straight from the pages of a picture book.

Dorothy Davis-Sellick

15

MY FRIEND SUZY

They laugh at me in the office
When I ring to let you know I'm on my way,
They know you never answer
It's just a game you and I always play.

You welcome me home with love and affection
Kiss me all over my face,
The house always neat and tidy
With never a thing out of place.

We enjoy going out for our evening walk
Down through the village, after tea,
Call in for a drink at the local,
Then back home to watch tv.

We get along well together,
Compatible is the word for we two,
Without you my life would be lonely,
I don't know what I should do.

You are my friend and faithful ally,
To me so honest and true,
A man could not wish for more loyalty
Than the loyalty I get from you.

You and I must tidy the garden
This Saturday if the weather is fair,
Digging and lawnmowers is something you like,
It's a hobby we both love and share.

If it's too hot for you in the car Saturday,
I shall leave you in the garden alone
While I go get the shopping
And you a big juicy bone!

Frederick Sowden

SWAN SONG

Above the sound of the traffic can be heard
The constant flapping of the wings of a bird
Perhaps it's trying to fly away
From the pressures of the day.

How sad and dreary this world would be
Without a blackbird singing in a tree
Or indeed the awesome sight
Of an owl hunting in the still of night.

As barns and hedgerows disappear
So our birds decline each year
Eggs are stolen from nests so rare
Does anyone worry or even care?

So right now let's make amends
And begin to protect our feathered friends
We humans, who think we are so clever
Should never forget, *extinct* is forever.

Jeanne Ellmore

THE ANGRY TIGERS

Trapped and killed ,
Just for the fur.
All for the coats,
That the rich ladies wear,

Tigers are angry
And so am I.
Hurting the animals,
And making them die.

Rhian Lovell

OLD DOG

Let your dog be
in the lea
of the mountainside,
let him bask
in the dust
of the lane
or seek shade
at the edge
of the summer -
green hedge;
let him stay
till the heat
of the day
has gone
from the sky,
let him be.
You will see,
he will know
when to go.

Geoff Fenwick

OUR FRIEND THE WHALE

Come listen to my tale
Of the graceful whale
She only has one plea
She wants to stay free

As she wanders through our seas
An awesome sight for all to see
But she's as gentle as a lamb
And poses not a threat to man.

She does not want to live in fear
Of the fisherman who are near
This gentle giant of the seas
We should listen to her pleas.

If you go hunting she will disappear
And there's nothing left for future years
Our beautiful whale will be extinct
Now tell me what will our children think.

C H Spurrell

THE TAKE OVER

So our territory has been invaded.
This meant for us our future's faded!
These lands had been ours for many years,
Now man has moved in, bringing many tears!
Their bulldozers have no respect for our home,
Ripping to bits the land that we'd roam!

We don't understand the monsters they've erected,
Do they realise how we have all been affected?
Man's compassion and greed never considered us,
They prefer to destroy than have any fuss!
Now we have to take our families and move on,
So invading territories where we don't belong.

Trying to find a way out of our situation,
Many are killed, crossing to the new reservation.
The hurt and the pain of leaving loved ones behind,
We must press on, for it's shelter we must find!
Sad for we must struggle now for our survival,
For we don't stand a chance against our rival!

Penelope Ann

CAT'S THOUGHTS

I am your devoted cat.
Slinky Siamese, elegant Burmese,
All those glamorous felines,
Would call me common.
My shadowy moonlight markings
Are black and white.
I am yours forever now.
I chose you specially.
You took me in from the frosty night
And gave me warmth and food,
When others turned me out into the cold
You showed me love, and gave me a special name - Katinka.
I have come to love and trust you in return,
for you respect my privacy.
You forgive my oft nefarious ways
When sometimes basic instincts may create in me
desire to stalk and kill my prey.
This brings you grief.
When for a while you go away
I grieve that you may never come again.
But I am waiting here to welcome your return
For I am your devoted cat
Katinka.

Mary Johnson-Riley

COW HIDE

Cousin cow in the British Isles,
I hear your life's endangered now,
once raised and fed and kept in style
it's changed - and how.

How fickle are your folks I think:
I hear they've lost all sense of life,
their values smashed, for just two pins
they'll have your hide.

And whilst I'm sacred here and pass
my days revered on the Ganges banks,
you're forced on trash and dried up grass
in cow-sheds dank.

Cow go hide, find a sheltered spot,
there must be some place out of reach
to shield you from their ugly plots,
some lonely beach?

Or a friend, a farmer who loves his stock,
a campaigner with a bit of land
who'll give you space and turn the lock
on MPs, banned.

Yes, have they brains, those human beings?
What vanity, their stupid pride,
making cash a God instead of Me.
Cow, hide.

Susan Biggin

SMUDGE FUDGE

My hamster's gone
From his cage
From his life
Big and furry.
Yet cute and
so very special.
Brown and white
Huge black eyes.
His squeaky wheel
So quiet now.
His yellow house
So empty now.

My hamster's gone
My room looks
Dull so different.
He was old
Two nearly three.
Fur was going
From his back
Like a human
Losing his hair.
No mucky sawdust
Or filthy bedding
Just a space
Plain and bare.

My hamster's gone
His climbing frame
His exercise ball
No use now.
His Christmas presents
His chocolate treats
Waste of money.
But who cares
He was mine
That means loads
He means loads
No other pet
Quite as great.
I'll love him,
I'll miss him
Forever to be!

Deborah Wood

THE EYES OF TRUTH

'Go, you pathetic creature!'
The kick was as harsh as the words
And staring into its eyes I expected to see
The same dull, robotic stare as were in the other's eyes.
But this one was different
This one held the truth.

There I saw the suffering and the bitterness
There I discovered the hurt and torture
Of a million animals rolled into one
There I witnessed the grief, dread and wretchedness
As it pleaded at my feet for the misery to stop.

This animal was different.
This animal spoke for them all.

Naomi Engelkamp

BORN KILLER, NATURAL HUNTER

Born killer, natural hunter
Sharpened claws
Mouth white with teeth
Eyes betray the wildness beneath.

Pursue, relentless for a prize
You wait
Hiding in the bushes
Waiting for the big rush.

To spring when the moment
Is perfectly right
Take flight from the hiding space
And eagerly give chase.

And if caught, this token
That you've sought
Who in vain from your paws
Tried to flee

Why, pussy-cat, oh why
Do you have to give
Your dead birds and mice
To me?

Gary Stubbs

A TOUCH OF MINK

Pinned without style,
Bobbing ignominiously against her shabby lapel,
Curiously unjust against threadbare tweed,
A graphic contribution to defiant pride.
Courtesy of a once bright-eyed creature -
And the fourth division scouts jumble sale.

Irene Hazell

DOLPHINS IN THE MIST

I receive no ability to trust
Like a child without security,

I receive no courage
Like a child without strength,

I receive no understanding
Like a child without sympathy,

I receive no space
Like a child without freedom,

I receive no choice
Like a child without options,

I receive no comforting words
Like a child without hearing,

I receive no eyes of future
Like a child without sight,

But now I receive time
Like a child with a chance.

Karen Cook

JUST ANOTHER GUN

It's just another hunter with a gun
Why do you hunt me, just for fun?
If you don't like me let me go
What will you do with me? I don't know.
My uncles my aunties, my mum and dad
The hunters are kind of driving me mad.
But then again I'm just a fox
That's meant to be in a box!

Danielle McMullan (Age 9)

VANTAGE POINT

Two magpies, high on the poplar tree
Thrush tries to feed from bird table,
More magpies lurk in sycamore at garden edge
(Tom appears) magpies chatter,
Squawk their disapproval.

The garden is still, but alive with the presence
Of menacing magpie
The sun is rising,
(Time to pour a cup of tea)
Sparrow tries to feed,
But magpies are lurking
The sparrow flies off at speed.

Sun now shinning on right hand fence
A magpie dances on lawn outside conservatory,
Flies off with foxglove in beak
Bumble bee takes nectar from standing foxglove
(Another cup of tea)
Majestic magpie feeds at bird table
(dustman is collecting at front of house)

Tom enters conservatory from garden and watches
Two bumble bees taking nectar from foxglove,
He and I observe the goings on outside
Tom returns to the garden,
Sits and watches a magpie feeding at the bird table
They respect one another!
(Tom climbs over fence and disappears next door).

Christopher R Smith

HEARTS OF GOLD

We should all respect our animals
and other people's too
Just because they're cats and dogs
they all have hearts, they really do.

They all feel pain, and fear and such
They all need love so very much
And when a dog will try to bite
Mostly he is filled with fright.

Don't buy a pet just on a whim
Lest long time care you give to him
You cannot simply turn him off
When you feel you've had enough.

You cannot go on holiday
or shut him up all day
He'll feel frightened, maybe bored
The lucky ones they are adored.

My own dear Ben died years ago
He was greatly missed and so
I wish that he could come and stay
For just one golden special day.

You do not know until they're gone
How empty life can be
Like living life without a song
That purring ball upon your knee.

So when you see an animal
Suffering and in pain
Help him please in some small way
You may not get the chance again!

Greta Edwards

ANIMAL CARE

Humans are free
they come and go
as they please -
They don't whine or bark
to be let off their leash-
But animals are dumb
and not born with hands,
They've to bark, whine whatever
to make known their demands.
So please stop and think
of their helplessness, despair,
Feed them, welcome them
with loving care.
They're part of God's planet-
and as He looks down from Above,
He'll bless you in abundance-
for giving them your love.

Mary Skelton

HARMONY

By example we can live in harmony
sharing the earth with animals who are free
Let us show others how to respect animals
Let us show others, the path, the way
by our own behaviour towards all creatures
as we respect and love them each day
Let us show others our respect for animals
as we live with compassion in our hearts
They will see by our example
and they will learn too - *to respect
and allow animals to be free!*

Yvonne Bowerman

28

A TIME FOR REFLECTION

The silent screams,
Which haunt my dreams -
A myriad creatures
In their death throes,
So entrapped in pain and misery,
They gnaw at bloodied limbs
To free their ghastly woes.

And can it be that man,
Could one day change the plan
Away from his false avarice
And become, like a child,
A creature of the wild,
To understand at last
His own unworthy prejudice?

The trapping of migratory birds,
Hares coursed; fox and stag pursued,
Bears tortured; badgers baited,
Magnificent whales harpooned,
God's gentlest little ones molested
To death in a foreign land
Where the angry bull's blood reddens the sand,
Elephant and rhino may soon be extinct
In the space of God's eyelid blinked!

Oh, man, what then will your children see?
They shall inherit only misery.

Julia Eva Yeardye

HAMSTER

Dark gold fur-ball.
Softly plump and sweet.
Eyes meet mine - up she goes
Scant pinkie tail exposed
Back feet slip on cold footholds.
Nose through bars expects reward.

Minute golden monkey.
Back feet cling,
Front feet swing to reach the floor.
Spreadeagled batlike
On the bars, she freezes,
Black ears curved to catch the sound
Of distant water, running.
Eyes brilliant, dark.

Wild.

Felicity M Bradley

OUR FRIEND JOHN

Our friend John has left us for a few days,
Kennelling with other neighbouring dogs.
Absence makes the heart to ponder.
Where has his warm shadow gone,
The one that stuck closer than a brother?
He'll be weaving his walk just now,
A pattern and a presence taken for granted.
His lead is an unseen thread of affection
Stretching through thickets, curling round hillocks,
And drawn back as day follows day by the pull of home.
No need to ponder his presence.
The unseen thread that brought him back
Holds us both in its warm embrace.

J H Scott

THE ALLEY CAT

It moved slowly almost squatting on its hind legs
Eyes glimmering, blinking with fear and agony;
This was the last life of the nine already spent.
The mighty cold spat its anger in convulsive rage
As the rib cage came under constant heavy fire
From the hail that poured down like crystal bullets;
The alley cat with the cute face sounded its last meaow.
It was dying, as the smoke from the chimneys burst forth
Through the icy air forming thin breath-like clouds,
Vanishing into empty space, freezing the frosty lights.
It searched for shelter, crawling cautiously, hesitating awhile,
Its numb paws trembling, shaking away the gelid waters.
It tried hard to find that swift-perfect-balanced-agility
Which had saved its life so many times in the distant past;
Now the strenght in its muscles was ebbing, fading fast.
It moved on, inch by inch, breathed its last. Darkness closed in.
The rain drizzled to a stop. There was no sound to stir.
The plate with the food on the doorstep remains untouched;
The alley cat will never again rub against my legs, never again,
But wherever it lies, there is no more suffering or pain.

Raymond Fenech

HUNGER

Ice frozen oceans,
Hungry seals cry for food
Starvation kills all.

But hunger is not the real enemy
Man is worse.

Candy Pearson & Alexa Rees

BONNIE

(From her friend Joan)

Bonnie my braveheart
The love of my life
Bonnie the guide dog
I'm guiding you now

You worked for us humans for many a year
Your eyes giving freedom
To those who couldn't see

Bonnie Oh Bonnie, growing now grey
Your legs are unsteady
Your eyes not as bright
Your heart full of love
Burning so bright

The shimmering curtain soon to fall
My beautiful dog is going home
Bonnie my Bonnie a far better place
I'll see you soon and we'll walk again.

Elsa M Summers

IN THE PALM OF MY HAND

Such a sweet little fledgling, you flew from the nest,
I was out in the garden, taking a rest,
Why in that instant you suddenly flew,
All covered with down, all fluffy and new.

All of a sudden my dog came to be,
He pawed you and turned you, under a tree,
A shout and he stopped, but the damage was done,
I lifted and looked at my sweet little one.

You snuggled right into the warmth of my hand,
Beak gaping open, a new friend you had found,
The sun beamed down on you newness sublime,
Freckles and spots in the beam all ashine.

I knew that your life was in minutes to end,
How glad it was I in your death throws, your friend,
One last struggle, you made a last stand,
Then your head came to rest in the palm of my hand.

W Curran

LEAVE US ALONE

I can hear the shot as it blows past my ears
        I can taste the salt from my droplets of tears
I run oh how I run through the grass and the trees
        My legs feel like jelly my lungs wheeze and wheeze

I puff and I pant and I make it back home
        My young ones are waiting they were all alone
I try to stay calm but I am shaking in fright
        I tried to assure my little ones everything is alright

Man has a gun for a fox that's not fair
        No animal is safe they can capture you there
They want our fur and for women to look nice
        But for them to look beautiful we pay the price.

I try to be cunning but that's not always to be
        We want to be able to roam and be free
I try to be safe for my cubs to grow strong
        I have to protect them but forever, how long?

They want our fur - to make collars, a new coat
        How can you wear one of us round your throat
We are far more beautiful wearing our own
        Why can't Man just leave us alone?

Lannette Lusk

ELEPHANTS WITHOUT TUSKS

I see elephants
By the hundreds.
Dancing, prancing, just lazing around,
Sitting drinking water.

You see their tusks
Shine in the light
The huge, smooth pointed tusks,
Which bring animals to life.

But what can I see, over there?
A man dressed all in green
Oh no! What do I see?
A gun, knife, Oh what?

He's gone now
But there's nothing left
Not a single herd
Those big gentle animals, dragged away from their tusks.

How quiet it is now
I see nothing here,
Except . . .
An abandoned body.

Tamsila Ahmed

WASTED LIVES

The bodies of the cattle lay,
Why was it them that had to pay?
Slaughtered by some cruel man,
Then taken to a butcher's van,
Their destiny a dinner plate,
Would you like that to be your fate?

Abigail Long (11)

I DO LIKE TO BE BESIDE THE SEASIDE

I could see those sad little eyes through the bars,
Of the vehicles carrying the sheep and calves.

There must have been six or seven lorries go past the feet,
Of the protesters who lined the Brightlingsea streets.

It was a cold day in February but our spirits were just as high,
As we stood in front of those monster lorries and stopped them
getting by.

As they edged toward the port the police were getting strong,
Whatever tactics the protesters tried to use seemed to go wrong.

By now the dock gates were in sight with the trucks speeding through,
There were tears on the quayside as the animals went out of view.

The whole town remained united and excised their powers,
By holding up those ugly vehicles for more than four precious hours.

We the protesters will be back again tomorrow for another day,
But for the animals we said Goodbye to, won't, with their lives
they'll dearly pay.

Robert Coleman

LIVE EXPORTS

Calves torn from their mothers
and herded on trucks.
A journey to hell
So the farmers earn bucks.
Poor little creatures.
When will it all stop?
Politicians do nothing.
We must do a lot!

Linda Randall

35

ODE TO A WHALE - A TRAGEDY

While you and I are fast asleep
With all our troubles out of reach,
Somewhere at sea out in the deep
A ship and crew their harvest reap.

They care not for the sorrowful cries,
They hear not a mother's sighs.
To them it's just a lump of meat
When caught, and killed for man to eat.

They say the kill is like a sport,
The harpoon gun and ropes are taut.
The spear flies out and finds the flesh.
The whale calls out with its last breath.

Why must we, as Mankind,
Seek and kill what e'er we find,
Within the depths of the ocean deep
While you and I are fast asleep.
A mother weeps as her child dies,
Beneath those cold grey arctic skies.

We're said to have such intellect,
But when are we to show respect,
To the majestic might and majesty
Of the great king of the sea.

Lyn Symonds

WHAT RIGHT

What right has man to kill a living thing
Be it fish, animal or bird on the wing.

To neglect, trap shoot and spear
Man is the hunter he has no fear.

He doesn't think twice about baiting his catch
Animal against man there is no match.

Animals are killed to line someone's pocket
Ivory tusks wrenched from its socket.

Fur and skins dressed for people to wear
These magnificent animals soon will be rare.

 The hunter always returns he sweats and toils
To kill fish of the deep for cosmetics and oils.

So gentle and graceful these creatures are
They deserve the right to live by far.

Pull the trigger killing for pleasure
Bred for these purposes at man's leisure.

Soaring free in the clear blue sky
Not knowing their end will soon be nigh.

Fish, animal or bird on the wing
Man has no right to kill a living thing.

Jean Cumbor

ANIMALS

Inside me there is a rabbit
All calm and content
Hopping around and minding its own business.

Now there's a wild beast inside me
Sulky and unhappy
Killing things in its path.

Now there's a pig in me - a large pot belly
Snout full of food, wanting to cram in more
Now it goes, satisfied, to lay around.

Now there's a cat inside me
Purring, wanting to be loved
Wandering around looking for affection
Finally it falls asleep in someone's arms.

Inside me there's been lots of animals
all with different moods
I love them all
They're all me.

Rachael Louise Mudd

HUNTERS

Before the little fox-cubs arrive
all the rabbits, lambs and hares
lie in the fields of green
without any cares.

Then along comes a hunter
and scares them away
from the green, green fields
where the animals lay.

They all run away
but one gets shot.
The hunter takes it home for the dinner pot.

As the animals are hunted
the families shrink.
Then made out of animals fur,
is a rich lady's coat of mink.

Sarah Healy

A FOX'S TALE

Cries echo in the dark cold night.
Then in dawn's first grey light,
You make your entrance.
Body lean, you limp in pain.
Not for you green fields and wood.
Rubbish ridden wasteland is your home,
My dustbin is your larder.
Soon the diggers will move in,
Destroy your lair without a thought or care.
Build their houses where your young once ran.

Brother fox can smell the dogs.
Hear the bugle sound its knell,
Heart beats faster,
Legs begin to run and run and run.
Exhausted now and nowhere else to haste,
Feel the dying pain of man's disdain.

If not for the uncaring hand of man,
Then each could make their own great plan.

Christine Beebee

WHY?

Twelve animals are extinct today,
Some of them because of man,
But the humans don't pay,
Only the animals can.

These animals can never be seen again,
With anybody's eyes.
With our help, they could have been saved,
Here the sad truth lies.

Twenty-three animals are near extinction today,
Some of them because of man.
These animals on our earth can stay,
If helped in zoos by man.

Us humans pay for elephants to die,
For their ivory tusks we demand.
On the floor these elephants lie,
Wasting on the land.

Two of the endangered species,
Are today being kept in zoos.
What of the other twenty-one?
Their lives they have still to lose.

Please help these poor animals,
Just do the most you can.
These animals are our friends, our pals,
And can only be saved by man.

Deborah Wright

BADGER

The trap is now set,
the humans retreat.
All seems so normal
but under your feet
are springs, cranks and chains,
all covered in bait.
A death trap is ready,
now just a wait.
Here comes the victim
wandering round.
The trap clinks and snaps,
he falls to the ground.
The humans are drinking,
they laugh and play darts.
But he is just squealing,
he dies in the dark.

R M McAnulty

I SUFFER FOR YOU

Make-up on the counter in the lab,
testing on me, dib dab, dib dab.
On my eyes and all over my fur,
not even caring how much it hurts.

Make-up testing and I'm treated like dirt,
but to them it's just another day,
and I feel myself drifting far, far away.

The sleeping drugs are taking effect,
at least I don't feel the pain I detect.
Please take note of my desperate plea,
come and help and please rescue me.

Leyla Butterworth

41

WHAT A LIFE

The world contains animals and some humans too,
Our numbers are inferior, yet we're not in the zoo.
Or in cages, or in pens, or cramped like in a jail,
Many of them never get to see a country hill or dale.
Just the four walls of their crowded home,
And they have very little space in which to roam.
They don't travel except to their slaughter.
The food they eat is the same each day,
It's good and wholesome in every way.
So they grow big and meaty like the owners dream,
And when he sells them he gives a big beam.
Money in his pocket, food on the table,
To rear more animals he is now able.
Generation after generation grow up on the farm,
The lifestyle they live must cause them some harm.
Trampled on, run into, bruised in every way,
Yet there is no way out, so here they have to stay.

Melaine Ludlow

ANIMALS

Animals, animals everywhere,
In danger, at risk but nobody cares,
Tiger, baboon, elephant and ape,
wiped out, extinct, by the year '98.

More and more animals killed every day,
Why oh why must it be this way?
Savagely killed for the sake of their meat,
we wear them as clothes,
and think it's a treat.

So stop and think before it's too late,
Don't put the animal race at stake!

Laura Davies

WHY WON'T THEY LISTEN?

So frustrating,
So painstaking;
If they'd listen,
They'd hear us saying
All our reflections,
Our speculations.
Why won't they listen to
Our contemplations,
Our little dreams
And our little schemes?
If only they'd listen
To our little screams,
Of worry and anguish;
We won't relinquish.
Why can't they hear us?
Do they think we won't vanquish?
We will conquer one day,
And tell our thoughts in a way
That they will not ignore,
Like when our lives were shrugged away.

Tara Breslin

BABY RATS
(No experiments)

Baby rats, sit so still,
curled in a ball of two bodies.
A nose may twitch, sniff the air,
but return to secure warm fur.
A new home, fresh smells,
afraid, unsure, entwined duo.
Missing their family familiarities,
they huddle for love and the need to share.

Sharon-Anne Kennedy

BIASED

Why does the spider on the wall
Have such a power to appal
The dreaded cockroach we might shun
Yet view a ladybird as fun
Are furry things like pussy cats
Better than mice, or bats or rats?

It seems too simple to determine
Which creatures should be classed as vermin
The honey-making bee is fine
For wasps we haven't any time
Some would prefer all things reptilian
Consigned for ever to oblivion

The snake fills many of us with dread
But isn't it all just in our heads
Have we the right to make distinction
Drive certain species to extinction
Are furry things like pussy cats
Better than mice, or bats or rats?

Sandré Clays

PEACEFUL PANDA

Somewhere around in China,
there lives a lonely bear,
Its name is called 'Panda',
lives a life without fear.

With its black and white patches,
view in poor sight eyes.
Nature around it silently watches,
Eats sugar canes, sweet and nice.

Does not like company,
wants to be alone.
Lives away from family,
has its own home.

This lovely bear is a friend,
yet it is so distant.
Strives for itself to the end.
One day it could become extinct.

Jenny Cheung

MY CAT

She came to me as a stray
Looking for a home to stay
Where love and affection is given every day.
She was so thin, and the eyes were dim
She stalked around from room to room
And, from her look, she did approve.
I gave her some food, and then a drink
She looked at me, and gave a wink.
Then a box to lay her head,
But she preferred a cosy bed.
She sat with me upon a chair
And I did hear her, purr and purr.
The time has passed, and she has changed
Now she's fat, her hair it gleams
And from those eyes, all wisdom lies
She walks around with regal grace
Expecting all one's time, and space.
I am not sure, that she's all mine
For she goes away, from time to time.

Dorothy Trilk

THE WHALE

Surging through the turbulent waves
We travel, dodging spears and staves.
The great harpoons that pierce and kill
Taking our brothers to please Man's will.

We dive so deep that they can't follow
And we might live to see tomorrow.
Our tiny calves they fret and cry
As whaling ships above, pass by.

When Man had culled our dwindling herds
A few spoke out with angry words
And told the many countries killing,
To save our kind, Man must be willing.

Our world, our great domain, the sea,
One day was clean and clear and free.
But Man, again, with mad solution,
Deposits waste and dire pollution.

The whaling ships sail out no more
To spill our blood upon the shore,
But Man continues with thoughtless notions
To pour his poisons in our oceans.

Styrofoam, sewage raw and plastic,
Toxic waste. is Man's new tactic,
Pouring in with each new tide
Till there's no place for us to hide.

Our blood still spills, but now internal
We, who once were thought Eternal,
The toxins in our systems burn
And we still die, till Man can learn.

Then one day when our kind are gone
And oceans rot beneath the sun,
Man will say ' How did we fail,
To see that we destroyed the Whale?'

Patricia A Essex

FARMYARD CAT

He is the *king* of his domain,
He knows it, and he loves it.
Mind you, there are dogs as well,
Maybe two or three,
But there is only *one* of me.
Farmyard Cat.

The work I do, makes up for two,
For, whenever I'm around,
There's not a mouse at all in sight.
I've chased them all to ground.
Farmyard Cat.

Ma leaves the back door open wide,
And beckons me to come inside.
I like this bit, it is sheer bliss,
She strokes my head and gives me a kiss.
But, my forty winks are all in vain,
For next minute, I'm shoved out again.
Farmyard Cat.

But, I'm still King of my domain,
I *love* it here, so I'll remain.
Farmyard Cat.

Dorothy Campbell

MAN'S BEST FRIEND

A man's best friend
Of that there is no lie
So much of a companion
No-one could deny.

With big brown, sad eyes,
That help him always get his way,
So persuasive . . .
That to explain, words could not convey.

Keen to be close,
Keen to be near.
This wee dog . . .
That we all love so dear.

An inquisitive nature,
That's so hard to suppress,
As long as you don't try,
And put it to the test.

He's the first to investigate any peculiar sound,
But if there is any danger
He's nowhere to be found.

No matter how much he has to eat,
When it's your meal times,
You're sure to find him begging at-
Your feet.
An appetite that no amount can quell,
He stuffs himself until his belly
Does visibly swell.

When he's not eating or looking to eat,
You'll find him snoozing on your favourite seat.
When you get home he welcomes you with a hearty greet,
By barking and wagging his tail and running round your feet.

Stephen McGeeney

IN MEMORY OF A LITTLE STRAY DOG NOBODY WANTED

I am a little stray dog of no particular breed,
They tell me I'm a heroine, but to this I pay no heed.
For the story books say a heroine has always a loving heart
Waiting to welcome her home again to a warm and friendly hearth.
But I have no one to love me, no one to really care,
For my story is a sad one and really it's not rare.
If ever I had a family in the dim, dark, distant past,
All I can remember is fear, thirst and fast.
Nobody wanted a stray dog, particularly one in whelp
And though I ran from door to door, I pleaded in vain for help.
By the time the dreaded day came truly my need was great,
But nobody came to my rescue and I was just left to fate.
I thought of my unborn babies - a mother will always fight
To save the lives of her little ones - however appalling her plight.
So I dug a hole, by the sweat of my brow, a hole deep in the ground,
And there brought forth my family and fed them until I was found
A bag of bones almost starved to death, with several bundles of fluff,
Then the RSPCA were sent for - they are kind and gentle not rough.
My babes have now all left me for homes such as I've never known,
And so I ask, and so I plead, 'Will somebody give me a home?'
I may be only a stray dog of no particular breed,
But everyone says I'm a friendly dog and all my love is free.
For my heart is as big as the ocean and all I need is a lap
To lay my head on in worship, a bone on the floor and a mat.

Dorothy Ballinger

ANIMALS

At the very beginning of time God made the animals, each of their kind,
Tiny creatures and the large, then He created man to be in charge.

Each animal was left for man to name. But it wasn't long before He chose to
Sin and maim . . . the first animal was slain!
Now we kill to eat, and animals everywhere humans ill-treat.
Some once lived, thrived and fed, now they hang, lifeless, dead!

Young seals are clubbed to death, dragged crying from their mother's breast!
How can man look into the eye of a small seal pup that's about to die?

Whales are still hunted; some almost extinct,
But still the harpoon in flesh must sink we drag them thrashing still alive!
The sea, red with blood and the stench of death.
Will we continue to kill until there's none left?

Another beautiful monster we still pursue. The elephant must die, it is true
To satisfy man's lust for making ornaments from its tusks.
We kill, mutilate and destroy, the poacher still outwits the warden's ploy.

Real beauty comes from within not through testing cosmetics on animals'
                                                                    skin.
It's great to paint our faces and smell nice,
But not at this appalling price.
It's just plain insanity to hurt our animals in the name of vanity.

Tally-ho! It's the hunt. When the fox discovers he's not really free.
Chased until exhausted, unable to run,
Followed by the huntsman having their 'fun'. When finally he surrenders
They don't give up the chase, but tear him to pieces and spit in his face!

There's dogs bred for fighting, cockerels too.
Animals left abandoned who have not a clue.
And thousands left dying . . . yes all this is true!

So let's not forget the Lord loves them too;
And I believe He wants to express it through me and through you.
He didn't give animals a voice to complain,
Just put us in charge to love and to train.

Neville Hawkins

MAN MUST KILL

The baby seal is dying!
The hunters have arrived.
He huddles near his mother.
There's nowhere else to hide.

His eyes so full of sorrow.
No place for him to go.
His mother calls him softly
As she's dying in the snow.

Her body's growing cold now!
No milk for him to suck,
Men take his mother's body
Throw it roughly on a truck.

So small, a tiny baby.
He trembles with his fear.
Why did they take his mum away?
Why did they leave him here?

He suffered till his life was gone -
He lingered in his pain!
For man must kill, they always will!
Again! And again! And again!

Ann Anderson

THE JOURNEY TO HELL . . .

Bang! Chop! Off goes another one's head,
Three million calves are now dead,
No guilt left behind, no time to set aside.
They have no rights, no feelings, according to some human beings.

Why should they have to go through the pain?
More people should complain,
Not enough people care,
Not many dare or have the time to spare.

But the true fact is this, something which nobody can dismiss.
That once upon a time . . .
All animals could roam freely outside,
But now nearly all are caged up and trapped inside.

They cry out for their mothers in desperation,
Wondering what on earth has happened to civilisation.
Having to stand in darkness, unable to move,
Perhaps wondering what the hell they are trying to prove.

Praying that the torturous journey will soon end,
Before too many go round the bend.
They are pushed off the lorry, yet not many feel sorry.
They are unaware of what is to come, or what is going to be done,

But then as they get near, they start to really fear.
As they hear the haunting cries,
Not even enough time to say their last goodbyes.
Terror, shock are upon them, for they now see what is to come . . .

Having to listen, watch and wait,
Trapped in by the gate,
It is now too late,
They have no time to escape.

Rebecca Bulmer (Age 15)

RATTLE AND JOLT, RATTLE AND JOLT

'Where are we going, mum? Where are we now?
I need a drink, mum. I'm so very hot.
I want to lie down but there just isn't space
Why are we going at this frightening pace?'
Rattle and jolt, rattle and jolt.

'We're going to France, love,' so the driver said,
'I need one too dear, but we'll just have to wait.
Be patient, my lamb, we'll drink when we stop.
I love you, my precious, I love you a lot,'
Rattle and jolt, rattle and jolt.

'My little legs ache and so does my head,
I can't see the sun, and I need some air,
I'm really afraid, mum, I don't like the smell,
Please stop this truck, I don't feel well.'
Rattle and jolt, rattle and jolt.

'Lean up against me, and get forty winks,
(God in heaven, this is living hell,
Oh please teach men that You love us too)
It's desperately cruel what exporters do'
Rattle and jolt, rattle and jolt.

'We're stopping at last, it's very dark now,
They are dropping the ramp and driving us out,
Wake up my lamb, stay close by my side,
My precious, my lamb, please try to wake up.'
No rattle and jolt, no rattle and jolt.

No tired little bleat, and no little baa,
Just a little dead lamb who had travelled too far,
In a hot airless truck for far too long,
And I think it is all so terribly wrong.
To rattle and jolt, to rattle and jolt.

Mary Greaves

RESPECT

Respect for animals,
Don't make them hurt,
For they have feelings too,
They see,
They hear,
They live and breathe,
But what else can we do?

Help our friends,
Show them we care,
Otherwise it'll be too late,
For the animals will live no more,
Don't lock them in a crate!

Why do we rob them of their golden life?
For it's something we all should treasure,
Why are animals of exception?
Why not give them this simple pleasure?
Who are we to say which should live or die?
Who gave us this right?
Surely not you or I?
Or there would be no fight!

Joanna Atkins (16)

DOLPHINS

Walls of death drifting in the sea
Killing dolphins on their way
Thirty-seven miles long, taking up the ocean
Someone has to stop all this murder

It all started in the sixties
When the dolphins were getting caught
Just to get tuna
All this has to stop

If this is to carry on
They will become extinct
Millions of dolphins have already been killed
All this has to stop

Three quarters of the earth is full of water
Yet, men are still going on killing
Not knowing the secrets of the deep
All this has to stop

Colleen Gravell (14)

VICTIMS

Dragon, did you ever exist?
From Tiamet's womb mother earth sprang forth
Pursued by brave Sir Elsinor
Run through by hero George.

Serpent with your energy rising
You lead the spiral dance
Now you hide from foolish fear
Crushed beneath the virgin's foot.

Wolf, greatest of all shape-shifters
Hecate's dark champion
Hunted and hounded by man's evil gun
Wild wolf, werewolf, alone and misunderstood.

Arachne, lurking in dark corners
Ariadne, you spin the web of life
Rescued Perseus from the maze
But now you bury yourself, despised.

And still the crimes continue
In field and forest, in ocean, lair and set,
In the horror of crate and cage
In the torture of the lab.

Deidre Mary Boylan

LAYERS OF PAIN

I awake in the light and that's how I remain,
for I only see darkness just now and again.
And I live with five more in a cage built for two,
and I eat and I drink and there's nothing to do.

And I lay a few eggs for as long as I can,
for the gratification of my overlord - man.
And when the boredom's too strong I peck at my friends,
for we're all just a bunch of naked nerve ends.

So I pecked and I pecked at my friend till she bled,
and I pecked her some more till at last she lay dead,
and man came along and took her away
and that's all that has happened in another long day.

But I won't peck my friends, not ever again,
and it takes me some time to eat up my grain,
for a man held my beak to a hot iron stay,
now my beak it's half gone, he burnt it away.

I'm a battery hen and my life here is through.
It is short and it's ugly, and it's all down to you.
I've suffered my life to make man his profit,
when will *you* stand up and shout out to stop it?

I awake in the light and that's how I remain,
for I only see darkness just now and again.
And I live with five more in a cage built for two,
and I eat and I drink and there's nothing,
there's nothing, there's nothing to do.

Phil Manders

TANDEM

For scores of years my wife and I
Pleaded in measures meet
For all creatures that swim and fly
And pass on padded feet.

In ballad, sonnet, lyric, ode,
Epic, haiku and ditty
We tried to lessen our brothers' load
With soft appeals to pity.

Like music poetry has charms
To teach the savage breasts
To treat the beasts of fen and farms
As our terrestrial guests.

With modesty it might be said
We ringed the world with verse
In hope of touching hearts of lead,
Converting the perverse.

We feel it will have been worthwhile
To prompt the muse we share
To cry out for the crocodile,
The horse and hunted hare.

Liam Brophy

EDDIE (THE EARTHWORM)

Eddie the earthworm is my name,
I've just been trodden on, I wonder who is to blame.
All you humans with big clumsy feet,
don't look where you are going when you walk down the street.
I've got a headache, and it hurts like hell,
and there is a bump, and it's starting to swell.
Humans please think of creatures like me
and open your eyes so you can see.
I am so little, so look on the floor,
I don't want headaches or bumps anymore.
Put me in your garden, and I'll work for you
Looking after soil is what I will do.
I will eat them bugs,
I will eat them mites,
because I am Eddie the earthworm,
    and I have *rights!*

Lesley Janet Dale

NO MORE PAIN

To let it continue you must be insane
Don't let animals suffer in pain
Cannot you see we'll have nothing to gain
Let us all for animals have respect
And never again to ever neglect
It's the vanity of the rich and dumb
Whose feelings therefore must be numb
'Cause their greed for such things as furs
Makes those animals' lives greatly worse
Why be cruel, experiment and kill
It only will prove you're dumber still
To hurt the ones we love is crazy
Stand up, shout no, please don't be lazy.

Sophia Dawn Lune

ANIMAL RIGHTS

Animals can't talk to say how they feel,
they just stare at the misery they know is real,
experiments that cause them pain,
animals do suffer for our gain,
we must put an abrupt stop to it all,
the animal cruelty figures need to fall,
just imagine ourselves in their place,
I'd much rather suffer than see the pain on a puppy's face,
Let the experiments be carried out on me,
I want to prevent animals' misery,
hold your arms open wide to animals near and far,
we need to show how kind we are,
animals like children need all our love,
let's stop all this now like we know we all should.

Claire Young

NO RESPECT FOR ANIMALS

Plodding on
life goes on
No room to spare
Habitats bare
life is cruel.

Man follows man
No respect at all,

Days and days
the same cruel ways.

The same ways of man
has destroyed all
kinds of life.

R Ellis

WHY?

Why is there no respect for animals
        or even our mammals?
Are we far superior than our four legged friends?
Is it because they are unable to speak their *minds?*
We as humans tower over them, scream and shout and leer
        they obey out of *fear*
Love and kindness that's what they need to feel.

We think the birds and bees are *free*
        'But are they really?'
We pollute the air they breathe.

We think the fish do not get harmed
But what about radioactive waste?
We know that's dumped out of haste
Surely that should raise some alarm?

All alarms should sound loud and clear
Cruelty to animals should instil fear
A heavy fine or punishment should fit the crime.

Why is there no respect for animals
That God has given so freely to you and me?
Why are they beaten - starved and shot
        to become a trophy?
To decorate a wall or desk
For someone to admire, and even praise
The person who caused the hurt and pain
        dear God what a terrible *shame!*

T J M Walker

TIGGER'S FAREWELL

It was a gloomy day,
My friend called me from downstairs, his voice was sombre.
I got out of bed, rubbing my eyes,
As I found my way to the dining room.
There on a sofa lay Tigger, motionless.
I froze as I neared the 18 month feline,
He had become such a part of the family of four.
His little limp body, now cold, sent shivers down my spine.
His brother and mother sat together,
Looking on, their faces seemed to comprehend what had happened.

I wanted no visit to the vet, a phone call would suffice.
Just to determine what may or may not have been the cause,
Of Tigger's premature demise;
A place was made ready under the rhododendrons,
Next to my beloved Siamese, Mimi.
He was peacefully laid to rest.
My eyes remained moist for the remainder of the day, recalling,
How my handsome little grey tabby, had been such a joy to have around.
The walks we'd take across the fields, to the oak tree.
Mimi, Clementine the mother, Woots his brother.
There was a pecking order, senior cats always first, the younger knew
their place.

I couldn't find Clementine or Woots anywhere, later that day,
I went to look in the bedroom,
There, huddled together, under the dressing table, the two of them
had stayed,
Probably coming to terms with their loss.

Amanda-Lea Manning

RESPECT

Although people puzzle the 'meaning of life',
no-one has realised the question,
most feel theirs the most relevant life.

Self and others - all we know

Does an animal have a self?
Some say no -
but make an exception for their pets.

Generally, should we kill the animals?
Is the meaning of life to protect the world?
Does the world include the animals?
We kill the animals for pleasure and profit
not from necessity.

Wasting life
Wasting the world.

Laura Stamps (16)

WHERE IS THE LIGHT

Another day dawns the sun's shining bright,
but wherever we look we see no light.
We know at the docks down in Dover,
Calves, sheep and pigs are sailing over.
Oh Lord in the Heavens hear our prayer,
it is so cruel they shouldn't be there.
Three days on the move no food or water,
taken to foreign ports ready for slaughter.
If not to be slaughtered, their short lives will be,
spent in a veal-crate, *what misery.*
Please dear Lord put this wrong right,
only then will we be able to see the light.

M S Pearson

EVERY BIRDSONG

All you who are alive,
know this song still survives.
All around you it's hummed,
sampled, whistled, drummed.
Catch it if you can.

All you who would chain me for pleasure or profit;
all you who would change me, twist and mangle and corrupt me;
all you who would cage me, try to swipe the sky from me;
all you who are playing,
catch it if you can.

All you who would use me, sacrifice me for something ungodly;
all you who would abuse me, not allow me to be;
all you who would rip me from my own flesh and blood, see:
all you who count yourselves in,
catch it if you can.

All you who make excuses by trying to downgrade me;
hear me once, and remember I am
the singer of the song,
catch it if you can.

The singer of the song, and the song sings me.
It sings, 'whilst you oppress you shall never walk free'.
It shrieks the shrill of suffering, and the threat of its clasping your throat;
it pipes the promise of liberation - worlds of joy in every note.

All you who play at life,
catch this song if you can
but don't try to chase it: down your weapons, understand
that this song is in every bird's call;
in every pig's snort;
in every fish's whisper,
this song can be caught.

Rupert Owen

BEEF - TO EAT OR NOT TO EAT!

The healthiest, happiest farmyards
Must surely be organic,
Other animal husbandry
Could be a cause for panic!

Instead of lush green meadows
With contented cows a-grazing,
They're confined to sheds with sheep-based food,
Which really is amazing!

Cows, sheep and pigs aren't cannibals
To have to eat each other,
Their bodies all are structured
To eat a natural fodder.

To tamper with what's natural
Can be a serious matter,
Pursuing wealth and fortune
With wallets getting fatter.

Bending all the rules to suit
The selfishness of man,
Has rebounded on the human race,
We're carrying the can!

Disease has incubated
In animals for eating,
Passed onto human beings,
And this may not be fleeting.

It may be few, or many,
At this stage who can tell,
But through mankind's misusage
These animals now face hell!

Valerie Jeffery

DAY OUT AT THE MAKE-UP FACTORY

I woke up, squashed, uncomfortable,
It's dark, someone is carrying me.
I can't see my children,
Where am I going?

Bang, I've been dropped,
My head is heavy.
People glaring at me,
What is happening?

For a second I thought I saw other dogs.
Saddened and mournful faces.
There was something different about them,
They were dead.

I was thrown into a cage,
I could hardly move.
I was alone.
Where were my owners?

Someone came for me, grabbed me by the neck,
I backed away, but it was no good.
My piercing scream was the last thing I heard.

Sophie Coulton

BORN FREE

When you sit down to eat your meal,
Please remember how they feel,
for them it's not a happy life they lead,
but one waiting for our human greed,
Such despair, how unfair
Set them free like you and me!

Rebecca Leed (14)

THE BATTERY RUN . . .

You stand, feet on wire,
cramped, surround.
Day in, day out
month in month out
prisoner.

De-beaked, plucked and raw
squashed, within a small wire cage,
with three inmates.
Doing time
passing time
laying eggs.

Stripped, of all natural urges,
an egg producing machine . . .
alongside
the metal sizing and grading machine
production within production.

Smelly, noisy, dark and long
your corridors spread.
Bars in front, behind and to the side.

Replaced eventually,
by wooden crates.
Dazed and blinded by daylight
that is strange.

Piled, six high on the lorry
to the slaughterhouse line.

The battery run,
or, as the farmer
predicts,
production output high . . .

Jaine Wild

RESPECT FOR ANIMALS

I may have four legs, where you have two,
but I have feelings just like you.
Pain can be felt by one and all,
human or animal, big or small.
Some of us are shot, just for fun,
some the hounds have on the run.
Some are shut up, and moved in vans,
to find our fate in foreign lands.
If man was beast I wonder if,
they'd understand we want to live.
They'd see that life is a precious thing,
they'd see that happiness we could bring.
Some of us do have a happy home,
we're lucky to have love shown.
But why o why is it so hard,
for them to respect us for what we are?
Respect is just a little word,
and even if it sounds absurd,
please give us some if you can,
then we can live at peace with man.
God's world is home to everyone,
He wouldn't like what's been done.
But respect for all of us would be,
the start of humanity.

Joy Cox

CONSIDER

My son! No, no they're taking my son!
I've been so blind, I didn't realise.
Resist! I can't, I'm powerless,
I implore him with my eyes.
Trying to find a voice.
Used and confused, my son . . . my life,
Bring him back, bring him back!
You don't know . . .
A whirling void is mine.
Images now, the barn
Where I sheltered with you
From the storm, my firstborn.
Thieves, murderers, murrain!
And again, despair.
The pain, concealed, I signal
'I love you' and wheel about.
My heart slashed and halved.
My son, my own son.
My calf.

Wendy Hickinson

MAD COW

One cow after another
Fight to get their feed
What a price to pay
To satisfy their greed.

The crushed sheep carries the germ
They give it to the cow
The farmer then sells the meat
Look where the germ is now.

The government say it's safe
Yet no-one will buy the meat
The government want to fight
But how could they compete?

When will it finish?
Will it ever stop?
Will we all become vegans
And give meat the chop?

Jodie Davies

ANIMALS

The animals in the wilderness,
The mammals in the sea,
The lions in their cages,
Why can't they just be free?

The monkeys of the jungle,
The birds who own the sky,
They should be able to swing from tree to tree,
And fly in the sky so high.

We people take it for granted,
That the animals of the land,
Should be able to live their lives to the fullest,
And to roam the earth so grand.

But the animals that we dream of,
Don't live their lives so true,
They die horrid and dreadful deaths,
Or end up in some zoo.

I think the animals of the world,
Should live their lives with joy,
Not to be caught on a fisherman's hook,
Or to be a rich man's toy.

Carly Rodgers (14)

UNTITLED

Don't just stand by and cry while they die.

Do you know what you eat
what you wear on your feet,
Do you feel no alarm at the harm
of the factory farm,
Does the gain outweigh pain
when they're slain?

What about the despair
of the poor caged bear,
Or the children who're taught
that to kill is a sport,
The horse made to run to his very last breath
and the donkey who simply gets worked to death.

For scientific skill we torture and kill
steal parts of their bodies whenever we're ill,
Is the reason we find that the whole of mankind
must be blind and out of its mind
Or, has someone the courage to stand and object
before it's too late please show some respect.

Don't just stand by and cry while they die
            Object, protect and respect.

Fay Gordon

FREEDOM

A bird must fly freely.
Take away its freedom,
And you take away its wings

Claire Angharad

A BATTERY HEN

I am a hen,
Kept by men,
In a cage for all my age,
I have to sit in my own dirt,
My feeble body is squashed and hurt,
Thousands of others are the same,
Living a life full of suffering and pain.

Lucy Roberts (13)

NIGHTMARES

(This is how I feel about live exports)

My nights are restless I rarely sleep
I think about the calves and sheep,
are they safe are they well,
or are they on the road to Hell.

The sadness these shipments cause me
no-one will ever know,
I hear their plaintive crying
It reaches deep into my soul.

The keepers of the planet know
that I care for the animals on the earth below
I want to see them where they should be
out in the fields, alive and free.

I will fight on for the battle's not won
and I'll shame the exporters one by one,
I live in the hopes that perhaps one day
the last transport lorry will soon fade away.

M Pearson

A DOG IS FOR LIFE

I was playing with my brothers and sisters
one day, when a man came and took me away.

He left me in a cold dark shed . . .
for a long time I wasn't fed.

The next day he came and pulled me out,
and then I heard a little girl shout . . .
'Puppy!'

For a while the girl fussed over me,
and at last I was given some tea.

An hour later though she went out to play
And that was the last I saw of her that day.
When she got home she gave me a pat,
Then I was pushed outside on a mat.

Two days later the girl said
she was bored with her pet,
And the man said
I was getting him into debt.

So one week later here I lie,
in the street.

I don't know why.

Rhiannon Williams (11)

SPECKLE'S POEM

Everything started
In the year '91,
When we learnt of the plight of the greyhounds,
And what had to be done.

It was in an article
In the local newspaper,
That we read about Speckle,
Who was to be our dog later.

They mentioned many dogs
That needed a home,
After being raced on the track,
And abandoned . . . alone!

Speckle came to our house
On the seventh of December,
And we could tell in his eyes,
That being mistreated is what he remembers.

But now he enjoys living
As part of a family,
Including three cats,
And Benjie the Yorkie!

So if you have a home
In need of a pet,
Give a greyhound a chance,
To be loved - no regrets.

Natasha Kemp (14)

THE FOX

Why was I created, why was I put on this earth
chased by dogs and horses, is that my special worth
If I was killed for the table, served with thanksgiving and grace
but ripped up by a pack of hounds, just to put a smile
on someone's face
the world is my hunting ground, this fact is true
work hand in glove with nature, I will give my services
to you
Killing and culling is my job, that's why I am called a pest
Don't blame me for the way I was created, for I am only
doing my best
be responsible for your stock, keep them behind
locked doors
remember you would do the same thing, if you
were walking in my paws
being rejected and persecuted, brings a tear to the eye
it made me very frightened, and that's what made me sly.

T M Allbright

RABBITS!

You're cute and fluffy
And soft to touch
Your house is a little
Wooden hutch

When it's warm
You come out to play
But when it's cold
You go to sleep in the hay

Your paws are small
Little balls of fluff
And your tail is a
Powder puff

In the garden
Deep holes you dig
Your teeth are sharp
And your ears are big.

Debbie Carlin

THE HUNT

Pompous hunters upon horseback -
Any sign of feeling they do lack,
An innocent fox they're out to kill,
Slowly, painfully - all for the thrill.

For miles and miles the fox is chased
As by a pack of hounds it's raced
Through the wood, across the land
No longer can the fox withstand
The exhaustion of a hopeless run
For him the hunt holds no fun.

The death is slow as painfully
It's ripped apart barbarically.
The hunters watch with laughing eyes
As the fox needlessly dies.

I can't believe it's considered leisure
To kill a fox for morbid pleasure.

Cleo Fychan (14)

MISTAKEN IDENTITY

The night before I dreamed a dream where heaven came in view,
And the soul who came to meet me I already felt I knew.
He said 'I am spirit animal and their many forms I take,
And in how man's come to see me he is making a mistake.

You mistake me for an object, you mistake me for machine -
You forget the wonder and the beauty you have seen.
You mistake me for a product on a conveyor belt -
You forget the contact and the friendship you have felt.

You hunt me down to rip me up, and this you call your fun,
You put me in a tiny box and hide me from the sun.
You steal my young and kill them, keep me breeding constantly;
Freedom means so much to you but I'm in slavery.

You inject me with diseases to study my demise,
You fatten and force-feed me till I'm twice my normal size.
I'm sent for execution, into the trucks I'm thrown;
How can you buy and sell that which you never truly own?

How can you make a profit from the loss I have to bear?
Don't you think I suffer? Is it easier not to care?
I just died a million times - I just died a million more;
Will you ever face the truth of what my pain is for?

That money's put ahead of life; the life that cannot talk,
The life that can't complain, or from a prison walk:
That greed and power merge in man to take my liberty.
All I ask of you is that you have respect for me.'

Janet Nunn

TORTURE CHAMBER

Stopping to look at the map in a gateway
I saw a movement out of the corner of my eye
There was something I did not care for in
The huge iron gate
The aggressive 'keep out' notice
The badly drawn picture of a pig's white face on the wall
Announcing the livelihood of the
Inhabitants of the house.
I looked closer at the movement and recoiled.
A huge pink-brown pig with turned-up nose
Was stuffed into a tiny metal container.
There was a bar in front of its nose.
Its mouth was open as it ground its gums on this bar
Raw and red with chewing.
Why was it there?
How long had it been there?
How much longer would it be there?
My whole soul felt pity, anger, indignation.
I wanted to go and set it free.
I felt impotent, helpless and still now when I think of it
I feel churned up.
One telephone call produced 'what you or I think of as
Cruel is not counted as cruel legally.'
If this, I ask, isn't cruel, then what *is?*

Gillian Service

UNTITLED

You don't see their faces cowering,
away to the back of their cages,
The noise of poor animals screaming in
so much pain from being burnt, starved,
poisoned, injected, stuff being poured into
their eyes, How can you say this is
justifiable in 1996?
Locked up in the secret labs not
seen or heard,
But only *we* have the power to be
their voices,
So this story that I have told,
can be history.

Unlock the labs.

Lisa Hammond (17)

INNOCENT PRISONERS OR CRUELTY

The death lorries roll up,
            Again and again,
Calves torn from their mothers
            In terror and pain.

Their nightmare begins,
            This journey of shame
Dragged onto boats, their last look
            at the sky,
Little do they know
            they're soon to die.

All they ever wanted was to romp
            and play,
Not to end their lives in this cruel way.

Mary-Lua Colverson

DREAMING ON THE STREET

Please Sir, before you pass us by,
Give us a bit to eat.
Please Ma'am, when you go home,
Bring back some water to drink.
If you can little girl,
Tell your mum about us.
Maybe she will come and help.
You see, I've been a dog on the streets for years,
And still I long to lay by a warm fire at night,
With a boy, a little boy or girl, who would play with me.
A regular meal, of meat or fish,
To look forward to every morning and night.
Strokes and cuddles, and walks on a lead, would be my daily treat.
I dream every night that a family would rescue me,
But I know that will never happen.
I know that instead of meat, I'll always get bones,
Or any other sort of food that I can find in the dustbins by the homes.
I'll never get to be stroked and hugged by a little child,
Instead of being kicked out of the way by a protective father,
Who thinks I would hurt his child.
Instead of walks, I'll have to run from cars and humans,
So I don't get kicked or pushed out of the way.
So next time you see a dog,
Running loose on the road,
Look into its eyes, and remember what I said.
It is not a useless thing, with no feelings,
It's a heartbroken animal, who hopes you will help.
Don't ignore him.

Laura Chenery (13)

THE ONE PER CENT

Just one per cent of stuff genetic
Makes us Homo Sapiens -
So akin we're to our athletic,
Furry brother, Chimpanzee!
We look through a distorting lens
At him - may even laugh - and miss
That strange communication in his amber gaze.
It speaks to us of Eden-days.
We see him through a glass, myopic
Stripping him of earth-born magic
That links us in a deep blood-kinship.
But is not pride a mite pathetic
And scorn and sophistry synthetic
For Homo, wobbling nervously
Atop old Darwin's Animal Tree?

Caroline Taylor

PAIN

No-one can feel the pain I feel,
Cramped, squeezed and shivering.
Why, why should I have to die
for man's greed?
I can't feel my legs,
Where are my legs?
I'm dying of starvation,
I haven't eaten for days.
They're going to kill me,
I know they are.
They've killed him,
my brother is dead,
It's me next I know it is.

Hilary Beevers

GIVE CREDIT WHERE CREDIT'S DUE

Give the meat eaters some credit
for when they say they 'like the taste'
they're not so stupid or pathetic or unintelligent
that they mean they're murdering innocent animals
to stimulate just one of their senses . . .

What they really mean is
they like to *smell* the death
see the blood
touch the rotting decay
and *hear* the tortured screams

as they *taste*
the *screaming, tortured, bloody, rotting,*
decaying, murdered dead flesh of the innocent
slaughtered animals that they like to refer to and think of as meat.

It's just that they have trouble expressing themselves.

Max

UNHEARD VOICES

Look out there, out into the open;
All you can see is green.
Look out there, out of the lorry,
To that place we've never been.
From birth to death, pen to abattoir,
All our lives we've been locked away,
And our murder goes on, year after year;
It seems this is how things will stay.
And they say that we're stupid, those humans
Who pack us off on this tortuous death-ride,
But there's one thing they say that they've got right:
The grass *is* always greener on the other side.

Jo Ritchie (16)

81

LIFE AND DEATH

As a man lifts a whirring chainsaw up;
The birds watch it cutting the wood,
Their home is reduced to dust
Money is made, roads and pollution are made
But precious homes are lost

Someone in a white coat calls himself a scientist,
He peers in one of the many cages,
Another chunk of fur falls out of a rats flabby red skin,
A pretty label is stuck on a bottle of baby lotion,

Chickens are cramped in small cages,
They peck one another until only a few
feathers remain,
It's dark, hot and the smell is revolting,
Eggs roll through bars ready to be packed up,
Soon to be labelled farm fresh,

A horse speeds on as the whip painfully cracks,
The gold buttons against a red jacket glisten,
Dogs race forward encouraged by cheers,
The fox begins to slow ready to
be ripped apart
My only wish is that us humans will
learn to respect animals.

Melissa Blewitt (16)

SCREAMS OF TORTURE!

I hear a cry
A scream of pain
An undying echo of endless torture
Then visibly I picture
a small defenceless creature

The crying becomes nearer
I now realise it's an animal in pain
A human cry is unbearable
but an animal's cry pounds through your ear drums.

I can't understand
why mankind can be so cruel
Killing for pure pleasure
shows you're in the wrong

So why not kill your own kind
and leave the helpless to tread this earth in peace.

E Snell (15)

THE PUPPY

A ball of fluff
Pathetic and small.
Huge feet that seemed to dominate
And cause him to fall
Spreadeagled on the floor.
Tongue all eagerness, searching
For food and love.
A face friendly beyond belief
Eyes longing to please,
How could I resist?

Wendy Gibson

THE EXPORT CALF

Your life is mapped out, you have no choice
An innocent player, without any voice

All you will know is what men decide
No warm, loving mother to nuzzle beside

Soon you start a journey, you are not very old
Firstly to the market, where you will be sold

After this trauma, at a lairage you stay
You meet many like you, but are not allowed to play

After such a short time, on a lorry you are loaded
Such rough treatment, you are kicked, pushed and goaded

Then a sea journey you have to endure
Bewildered and thirsty, you reach another shore

Your final destination, not a field but a shed
No fresh air, no grass, not even a bed

Six months is your sentence, they know you won't be freed
Your final act is a lonely death, to satisfy man's greed

Your life was so short, and so full of pain
Expected to give, but with nothing to gain

This is why we protest, our anger is rife
All animals should be respected, and given a decent life.

Patricia Thomas

LABORATORY HELL

Before me was the most awful
sight in the world.
For no words can describe the
horrors that would unfold.
A white rabbit looked at me
through his bleeding eyes,
of no use anymore was
abandoned, left to die.
There were over fifty cats with
numbers not names,
each had electronic gadgets
attached to their brains.
In front of me was neglect of
the largest scale,
but soon I realised that
my tears were of no avail.
The whimpering noise was a
terrible din,
every animal had bones jutting
out of their skin.
Two dogs in one cage, one
licking the other's head,
I took a closer look, the dog
lying down was dead.
I saw over a thousand
animals today,
scared, trembling, cowering,
each one of humans afraid.
The blood, the torture, the
chains cutting through their skin.
For each being an animal
was their only sin.

Carla Boreham (14)

DARK STALLION

Galloping wildly,
Heart beating.
The pounding of hooves,
Never fleeting.

Evil eyes,
Stone-like stare,
Fierce expression,
Always there.

Tough yet kind.
Strong yet weak
It is of the
Horse I speak.

Faster, faster.
Never slow
You don't have time
To let love show.

Joanne Harkens (14)

RESPECT

Respect is what we humans lack.
The weak against the strong.
And yet we are the only ones
Who can tell what's right from wrong.

We have no need to fight or kill
So we can stay alive.
But we still torture, capture and spoil
For what? Not to survive.

Our native ancestors understood
To take only what they need.
And it still could be like that today
If we could conquer greed.

Greed and ignorance, cruelty and fear.
How can we hope to protect
This beautiful earth with its wonderful life
Unless we learn to respect?

Linda Fernandez

DAWN

Now is the time to turn away from the west,
  the direction of darkness, death and black.
We must face the east,
  and the rising of the dawn.
We are at the dawn of a new era,
  one in which all of mother earth's creatures could and should
                              inhabit in harmony.
Why should we have the right to harm and destroy those creatures
                              who cannot fight back?
We must *respect* and care for them in these uncertain times,
  and make sure that we do not inflict any more pain than we
                      already have since our race began to dominate.
We have been carefree and cruel,
  not considering the serious consequences of our thoughtless actions.
We must unite as a species, as a part of nature, as a planet
  to stop the pain and torment.
Respect for our earthly charges is vital if we are to turn
          away from the cold west and towards the warmth of the east.
The east, the light, our saviour - *Our Dawn.*

Claire Walsh (15)

SILENT ANIMAL

Fear feels as pain,
The cold is nothing more than
a distant light.
The cries and agonies of cramped
crushed veal calves,
Petrified, transported from coast
to coast, trying to subdue their
terrifying journey.
The poignant misery of scarlet
coated foxes, torn from limb to
limb.
The ululation of bloodhounds
hunting the foxes' scent.
Silent yet salient noises of
zoo cages.
Locked away for ever to be
looked and laughed upon.

Kate Eves (14)

LONGING FOR LOVE

Surrounded by sadness,
a cage with no key,
no means of escape, no way to set free,

Long mournful eyes,
stare hard into space
A look of pure sorrow drawn over his face

Hungry and frightened
the poor pup doth cry
abandoned and lonely, just left there to die.

Amanda Doye (15)

ANIMAL TESTING

What is the point? I ask myself,
In putting the animals in bad health.
The animals go through so much pain,
The people who test just can't be sane.
A little rabbit with his innocent face,
All this to satisfy the human race.
Can't you see the suffering they make,
Just to help you look pretty and fake.
The little cages they are all squeezed in,
To me this really is a sin.
It is not right, it is not fair,
The pain and torture they have to bear.
So make sure the next perfume you get,
Is not injected into *your* pet.
Read the label before you buy,
Or you could be forcing animals to die.

Beverley Joyce (15)

DESPAIR

A calf, perhaps just one week old,
Is from his mother torn,
If he could speak, what would he say?
Why ever was I born.

To suffer hours of torment, in a
Crowded, stinking truck,
And then to spend six months of hell,
Standing deep in muck.

He hopes that death comes swiftly,
Did he hear someone say
The British they love animals,
But greed gets in the way!

Anne Travers

REMEMBER ALL SOULS

An animal can be your friend.
So please read on and you will see
Who could be your mate until the end
And how much better we all could be.

The next time you purchase eggs
Think back to those chickens' fragile legs,
Those crying eyes and soul that begs.
Just remember you ate that soul.

While grocery shopping look in your cart.
The animals you eat tonight once had a heart.
A heart that beats like yours from the start.
Just remember you are going to eat that soul.

When it is cold outside stop to think.
About that coat you are wearing - that mink.
If you cannot think like me, go and see a shrink.
Just remember you are wearing an animal's soul.

When you are out for dinner and eat lamb
Please realise all restaurants do not just serve animals in a pan.
Think twice when asked, 'What would you like, Sir or Ma'am?'

Your dog or cat is not like a fish.
Your 'pet' is swimming alone in a dish.
When asked if it could have only one wish.
It would say, 'Remember - I, too have a soul.'

Please think about the animals caged,
Most of what you see and hear is staged.
It is really much worse and I am outraged.
Remember - we all have a soul.

Ramona L Vorberg

ANIMAL THOUGHTS

We have no decisions to make, never given a choice,
Our fate is in your hands, we would speak out if we had a voice.
There are some people who care, who try to ease our pain,
But not everyone will listen, and it's often all in vain.
So many of us animals are in constant pain and fear,
When I see my friends so frightened, I often shed a tear.
If only man would understand, we have thoughts and feelings too,
But we cannot speak out for ourselves, we have to depend on you.
What have we done that is so wrong, for us to be treated this way,
For us animals to be treated fairly, oh how I long for that day.
There is so much animal cruelty, and so many people to teach,
But many close their ears, and keep well out of reach.
We really cannot take much more, it has to stop one day,
And each day and night I make it through, dear God, oh how I pray.

Lindsey Woods

TO A FACTORY FARMER

Think for once,
Think for real.
Change your life,
Change all lives.
Use your eyes,
Use your ears.
Hear the screams,
Hear the cries.

You can stop the pain,
You can stop the lies.

So this is someone's livelihood?
So was slavery,
But was it good?

Jonathan Briggs

91

THE VEAL CALF

Small, thin and lonely taken from its mum.
This poor little calf, he doesn't know what he's done . . .
Shivering and frightened pushed into a crate
Little does he know he'll end up on someone's plate.
He's compressed against the others, all on death's row.
He doesn't know what's happening, who is friend or foe.
Surrounded by angry protesters waving banners in the air.
Doing something about it, showing that they care.
The calf doesn't know, that they're trying to save his life.
He's oblivious to the fact he'll end up under the knife.
Life will soon be over for the poor little calf.
His life's been taken away reduced by over half.
He will be slaughtered, because of human greed.
For us to survive his meat we do not need.
Veal is eaten by people whose compassion has been lost.
The life that has been taken is worth more than the meat's cost.
How can this happen? Where's humanity gone?
Don't they understand that killing things is wrong?
When will it stop? When will they realise it's cruel?
When will there be a law? When will there be a rule?
What happened to love and respect, for creatures great and small.
It was just a lie, there's no respect at all.
But the day will come when animals will rebel, and vengeance
they will seek.
They'll make us pay for slaughtering their fellow cows, pigs and sheep.
Animals will rule, and we'll be their slaves and have to serve.
Then every human being will get what they deserve.

Sian Thomas

ELEPHANTS

Their deep dark eyes,
As deep as the sea,
Keep twinkling back,
They're looking at me,
Their ivory tusks,
Gleaming in the sun,
This dry hot weather,
Seems to be no fun,
Their big, long trunks,
Helping them to wash,
Helping them to eat,
To cool down in this heat,
Their big, floppy ears,
Twitching with the flies,
But now the heat has gone,
Clouds are filling up the skies,
The splashing of the rain,
Trickles down onto the floor,
The cracks are disappearing,
No heat to cope with anymore,
Into the cool water they lay,
Hoping the sun has ended,
And the water will last,
For just one more day.

Paula Salter (13)

SURVIVAL

Soaring above the tree tops,
Gliding like a kite in the wind,
The kestrel swoops and dives,
Scouring the ground for lunch,

A tasty morsel of mouse,
That would do just fine,
Or maybe an insect or louse,
Whatever I don't really mind,

Grateful for anything I find,
In this daily Survival Game,
Play not if you're weak or lame,
Running short of razor-like wit,
Or the attribute of keen eye,

A vision of elegance in the air,
Shatters as he touches down,
Savagely he devours it whole,
A defenceless and struggling,
Quivering mess of a mouse,

Lunch is done and over with,
Now it's time for tea I think,
For who knows when, or if at all,
My next meal will come and call.

Into the sky he launches again,
In such apparent innocence,
No shame or remorse does he show,
Not a flutter of conscience at all,

For this is the merciless Wild,
Where Eating is all that matters,
Where survival alone remains,
Their one shared common priority.

Asia

THE WHALE

Oh God of the sea
Your song calls to me
As an echo in the ocean
A song filled with love and devotion

Oh spirit of the deep
Who could kill one such as thee
Your hunter is the savage
You the spirit of liberty.

Ian Barton

UNTITLED

Stumbling, stopping falling and rising again
Two creatures made a painful way
Between rocks on the oil-thickened tideline
With useless wing outspread, one sinks down
'Gainst the body of a brother.
                              Not understanding.
The other flounders on, bill uplifted in mute appeal
As though to a heaven helpless 'gainst the will of man
With eyes unseeing, thick film making dark his vision
The webbed feet misdirected
Take him again to deeper slime
To join the other creatures of that sea, that must in turn
Leave the cool green depths,
To rise through that deadly surface.
                              Understanding not.
But I understand,
Feeling pity and sadness for the creatures,
That 'Owe not any man'.
I understand, and am filled with a dark, dark anger.

Winifred Brewer

WHY?

Why?
Do we treat the animals,
Of this world so, badly?

Research?
Of course we need it,
But what about the animals?
They have feelings too.

How,
Would you feel?
Locked up in a cage, day in, and day out.
Suffering.
That life is fit for no human nor animal.

We have justice,
They should have too.
Their lives are not fair,
Their world is full of fear.
Fear of humans, and what we do to them.

What about their homes,
That we are destroying?
The trees, rivers, lakes and fields.
Chopped down, polluted, dried up, and burnt.

I've seen the video clippings,
I've got the leaflets.
Why?
Why should they go through this torment?
Medical research?
Find something else to test on, not someone.
Not this Kingdom's animals.

R Montague-Ebbs

MY MISTRESS AND ME

She's putting on her shoes
And now her coat and hat
And now she's dropped the lead
It lies there on the mat.

'Of course I'm going to take you out
You lazy sleepy boy.
Jump to it and be smart
And bring your favourite toy.'

It's all right for her wrapped up in woolly tweed.
When I have to go in my birthday suit.
A woolly coat is all I need
'Twould make me look real cute.

'Whoops! I stepped off the path,'
'Sit' she shouts pulling me back,
'You have to stop, look and listen
And keep on the right track.'

I spot a pal across the road
I pull at my leash to greet him
'Come back you silly stupid dog
That hound would tear you limb to limb.'

I walk sedately by her side.
We walk for miles and miles,
Down the glen, by the sea, over the hill
And wearily climb stiles.

Home at last I'm tired out,
I'm ready for my bed.
A nice cold drink my favourite biscuits
Then I'll lay down my weary head.

Muriel Wheatley

MIRROR MIRROR . . .

Mrs Valentine sports a coat
That shimmers against the snow.
Silver beauty bonds with her
Fine skin. Peachy pink, youthful
With keen white teeth that
Bite into a bread stick at the Ritz
On Sunday. In the street the
Silver coat hangs politely,
Crosses the road obediently,
Enters the parquet floored apartment
And drops lifelessly onto the ottoman.

Pleasing tints are fed into the hair
Of Mrs Valentine, shocks of
Coloured light exterminate the old
With sharp transition.
A high price for a new creation
Which tangles in the wind
And will not be controlled.
The white Mercedes Benz
Winks with seduction, leather seats
And luxury, moves like a snake,
All speed and no effort.

A tiny piece of coat trapped in the door.
Mrs Valentine tut tuts, turns to see,
Then splintered glass and streaked fur.
One dead woman. Thirty silver foxes.

Nicola Simler

DO ANIMALS MATTER?

Do animals matter?
Yes they do,
They are just the same as me and you.
They have feelings just like you,
But you don't get trapped and put in zoos!

Do animals matter?
Yes they do,
They have as much right to be here as you.
Why should they have to travel in conditions inhumane?
Over to the continent where soon they will be slain.

Now after reading this poem,
Do you really care?
I really hope you do,
Because it really is not fair!

Ria Banscherus

RED

Red streak flying fast,
Rushing, tumbling, falling past,
Thudding, panting from behind,
Hear the trumpet call unwind.

Gasping, failing, slowing down,
Baying, calling from the hounds,
Strength runs out, the end has come,
Tearing, slashing has begun

In a corner fighting true,
Red coats shouting will ensue
'The fox is down' we hear
Ripping, slashing - flesh will tear.

Rikki Fanchamps

FARMING NOW

I looked for a young lamb
And what did I see?
Sad eyes in a lorry
Looking at me.
I looked for a chicken
And what did I see?
Just crates on a lorry
Passing by me.
I looked for a young calf
And what did I see?
Brown eyes in a lorry
Looking at me.
Gone are the green fields
Sun, wind and rain.
Now only cold floors
Darkness and pain.
So we must fight on
To get all this ended
To make sure that kindness
And profit are blended.
May God forgive us
The things that are done
To these small helpless creatures
'Til the battle is won.

D Meyer

ROVER'S STORY

They took me home, and named me Rover,
But soon my happy days were over.
I made a puddle upon the floor,
That's when they pushed me out of the door.
I was only a puppy, I didn't know
That the garden was the place to go.
I was put in the car and taken away,
On a cold and frosty winter's day.
They left me many miles from home,
Cold, hungry, frightened and alone.
When you found me I was weak and thin,
You picked me up and took me in,
Then you said that I could stay,
And I'll be faithful to you till my dying day.
But people should know that it's just not right,
To abandon a dog any day or night.
He needs food and water, a cosy bed too,
And has to be taught all the right things to do.
Be patient with him and quite soon he,
A good and faithful friend will be.

Ivy Neville

DOG OUR REDEEMER

Man boasts that he's made in the image of God,
I think it more likely that God is a dog.
Having slaughtered the wildlife all over the earth
Man created only this one thing of worth.

God in his heaven must stand there aghast
At the monkeys and beagles pinioned and fast.
Civilisation! No these are the sick
To torture such innocents for a lipstick.

Ronald Guest

101

HYPOCRITES

We're the hypocrites of all time
Our people and their favourite line, of
'They're different, couldn't eat one of them'
Plate piled high with mint sauce and lamb.
To please the bitter sweet of taste
the logic unconvincingly based
on nothing concrete, moral or right,
it's purely greed and power of might.
We cannot justify in words of truth
just that it seems socially uncouth
to eat the dog and tame the sow,
or farm the cat and love the cow.
'It doesn't work, it's plain to see,
it's just not right - it was meant to be.'

The fate of lessers under our command
and so we choose, based on our demand.
Our selfish glut and so called needs
companionship and heroic deeds.
Indulgence to the extreme with them,
but still we say what, where and when.
The others cooped, farmed and bred,
shot and fished - a price per head.
The treatment society could not allow
our dog, is life endured by the cow
'It's different though' we state again
and pat the dog . . . and pluck the hen.

Alison Hawtin-Dumbrava

OF COURSE WE'RE NOT CRUEL

Supplying you eggs from her own tiny pen,
Lives a cooped up and cramped little battery hen.
She hopes you enjoy them, she hopes you don't mind,
That because it's so dark here she's already blind.
She eats and she sleeps, and she lays eggs for you,
Because this is all we allow her to do.
She can't stretch her legs and she can't flap her wings,
But please don't be worried about these small things.
She tries not to comment on things as a rule,
But I'm sure that she wonders why we are so cruel.
And then there's a calf in a small wooden crate,
He cries for his mother, for him it's too late.
He's off on a journey, over land and sea,
In a crate that is not quite as big as he.
Cramped and alone with no food and no light,
By the time that he gets there he's no pretty sight.
But please don't you worry, now don't be a fool,
Why could this calf think that humans were cruel.
Come on let's be honest there is no confusion,
There's no other beast escapes our persecution.
For this is our planet, yes all ours to rule,
So it's true when I tell you of course we're not cruel!

R M Pengelly

CALLING OUT

Happiness would be freedom,
Free of aches and pains.
If only I could make the
Sky open up and rain.
At least it would be easier
Than trudging through the sand,
Or wearing out my feet
Across the barren land.

With my heavy load they beat me,
To make me go so fast.
When I reach my destination
I can put it down at last.
If I fall down in anguish
They will shout at me and bawl.
So listen to our protest
To answer our distant call.

Catherine Robinson (12)

MORE ABOUT CHLOE

Scimitar clawed
She balances on my neck,
Indifferent to my squeals.
With her limpid, amber gaze,
Imperturbable and unperturbed as glass
The predator purrs,
Regretting proper prey
But accepting
A secondary offering.
Then she sleeps
Smiling, content.

Sylvia Dewhirst

THE INNOCENT

What have they ever done to us?
Why should we cause them pain?
The slaughter of the innocent
This killing's inhumane.
All part of God's creation,
They're blessed with a life.
Of which they are entitled,
So do they have to die?
We wouldn't have to starve,
We wouldn't be in need.
There is many an alternative,
Should we all stop eating meat.
You wouldn't stew your pussy cat,
A hamster, you wouldn't eat.
What difference does it really make,
Be it, dog or sheep?
They're just like us in every way,
With so much love to give.
Stop murdering all the animals,
And please, just let them live.

Tracey Dawn Kyme

SLAUGHTER OF MY OWN CUTE INNOCENT FRIENDS

Each night the scraps of the day,
I take to the park at my home
cute little foxes I feed.
At first there were eleven
now they have dwindled down to three,
those trusting little creatures who ate just 3ft from me.
Some hard cruel people
have killed most of the creatures who ate 3ft from me.

Carly Mulligan

FIDELITY

How can you describe time in an animal
Not with a pun, nor with something nominal
Three decades I've had Dalmatians
A long long time, no imitations
The first named Charie was fair of face
The second Topsy, I could never replace
Talk about dogs with love and titbits
Dalmatian puppies have no limits

Coats like velvet, brown languid eyes
Loyal trusting, that's not lies
I could be crying with not a sound
As sure as fate over she'd bound
Instinctively knowing all was not well
Transmitting my thoughts she could tell
You can't put time on something so precious
Without saying, they get the message

My husband died she sat by his grave
Such a character, such a knave
Hours, days, seconds, minutes
True fidelity has no limits
What is time, merely illusion
Some might say just a delusion
In the cemetery there is no time
My dog, myself and all that was mine . . .

Jean Tennent Mitchell

BRIEF ENCOUNTER

Nobody had told the fox he was wild.
Sometimes just living out was very hard.
No dinner bowl put out daily.
No warm basket to curl up in.

People were there to be avoided.
Life was an exercise in survival.
Concealed through the daylight hours
He only found confidence in the dark.

Yet he craved shelter from the cold winds.
Shelter too from the worst of the rain.
He only wanted to find a little warmth.
There it was in a corner of my garage.
Feeling protected by the darkness outside
He lay curled up as would a family pet.

'How much nicer this was' he thought to himself.
I don't know how long the fox laid there.
If I had known he could have stayed.
I would have just parked in the road
And left him his precious hours of comfort.

He blinked in the headlights of my car,
Shook himself and then stood still for a second
Looking aggrieved at my sudden intrusion.
Then he sloped off back to the undergrowth.
Back to his life of opportune existence.

I could never enter his world nor he mine,
But for a brief moment I had known him
And I was filled inside with compassion.

What was a garage anyway?
Who needed it most?

John Christopher Cole

LOVE ALL ANIMALS

God created animals,
He left them in our care,
We should respect his wishes
And look after their welfare.
They cannot speak to let us know
If they may be in pain,
So we must list' to every cry,
And never ever feign
To sort their little problems
And everything they need,
For that is what we're here for
And we must always heed.
They show to us their gratitude,
Their kindness and their love,
So we *must* give them gentleness,
Through our Heavenly Father, above.

Doreen McDonald Banks

ROSY POSY

We buried Rosy Posy today
In amongst the daffodil bulbs
She was a little ball of fluff . . .
A cute kitten.

We put a name board on her small grave
And sprinkled it with scented petals
My brother and me cried because we will miss her
But we know she went to paradise.

Just because she was a kitten
She still deserved respect.

Kelly Morris (8)

108

RESPECT FOR ANIMALS

From the largest creature the elephant to the little mouse so small
I have always been an animal lover, in fact I love them all
Many people treat animals badly from the domestic to the wild
But I was brought up to have respect for animals right from a little child
Animals should be free to roam and live in their own terrain
But instead their enemy man, hunts them down again and again

Some animals suffer the experimental labs whilst others are hunted for
their skins
To make us fancy shoes, handbags and other ornamental things
Fur coats are quite a luxury the essential fashion wear
But how many poor animals have died for that to be hanging there
The ivory trade is big business providing more exotic gifts to buy
But how many of us think of the elephants robbed of their tusks and
left to die

We must make people realise, we must make people think
Before more of the world's creatures end up becoming extinct
This problem is getting serious, hunting animals is not a game
If we keep losing more and more species this planet will never be the same.

L A Brown

UNTITLED

In the rush of modern life,
what's happened to compassion?
While we search for money,
greed has become the fashion.
Animals may not have 'rights',
but they deserve far more
than a long and painful trip
before they reach death's door.

Julia Long

A PARADISE THREATENED

Beneath the trees in sunny New Guinea,
The birds of paradise dance in plumage bright,
Under the green, protective, canopy,
An unforgettable impressive sight.

Feathers of turquoise and gold streaked through with green,
A sequinned breastplate and a shining wing,
Flash through the dark leaves, when they strut and preen,
Their brilliant lustre seems a magic thing.

Especially to the forest dwellers there,
Christian converts though they well may be,
Still do they hunt these birds for plumes alone,
Nor are they stopped by any missionary.

Now feathers adorn men who crave the power,
Of paradise birds, to so dazzle a mate,
They weave headdresses hour by tedious hour,
Then wear them proudly, as they sit in state.

The coloured feathers do not glow and gleam,
When worn by men, instead of by a bird,
These stolen plumes do not give them esteem,
In fact they make them look rather absurd!

A man has limbs and hair and flashing teeth!
Can fight with weapons, learn to read and write,
He can paint pictures, make clothes for himself,
Why rob the lovely birds? It is not right.

The missionary should not merely preach,
Or else, dead images, are what is seen,
Care of environment, he too should teach,
Love what is now, not only what has been!

Kathleen Scatchard

NASTY

There is a lad,
A little cad,
Whose hobby quite revolts me.
I'd take no joy,
From any boy,
Who similarly acted.

He's rather small,
As I recall,
I hope he grows beyond it.
If he were mine,
The little swine,
His habit would be ended.

I'd find a way,
To stop his play,
If that's what you can call it.
He's acted so,
A while I know,
How did he ever start it?

I feel he's not,
Much kindness got,
For creatures large and small.
As when they die,
And peaceful lie,
He skins, and then he stuffs 'em.

Stephen R Ramsden

A FAMILY OF FIVE (+ ONE)

I'm a tiny field mouse, with a family of *five*
Sometimes I don't know how we survive
We live on a farm next to a wood and have no trouble stealing food
The only trouble is keeping alive, for me and my family of *five*
In the early hours we raid the kitchen table, from last night's supper
When we hear the farmer's footprints we're off like the clappers
If we sleep in the barn there are rats and cats, much bigger than
us, and the farmer sets illegal traps
If we sleep in the cornfield we take chances with our lives
The combine harvester doesn't mind what it slices
Or a friendly *owl* might swoop and pick up us mices
If we live in the farmhouse we're poisoned to death
Six little bodies can't bear to think of the mess
We've found a cosy corner in the hen hut, she even lets
us share her food
Our favourite is corn and sheaves of wheat more than enough
For us to eat, we roll the sheaves along with our tiny feet.
I suppose we're a nuisance as we make holes in things.
But I'm afraid that's part of the way we live
Life is a gamble every day, when I let my young uns out to play
Shep the old sheep dog he's a softie you know, when we're out
For a walk, he just watches us go
The farmer hasn't got a grandfather clock where we can run
up all day, from bottom to top.
Or wing on the pendulum till we drop off
So! One more day at least we've survived, me and my
Family of *five*
Life on the farm is safer for me, than my poor cousins
in a laboratory,
By the way the 'kids' are Hickory, Dickory, Dock, Mickey and Minnie.

Sandra Witt

TOP CAT DICKENS

You are my constant and much valued small companion,
Conversationally a raconteur of wit.
With a subtlety of tone, ranging from a friendly moan
To soprano's screech enlivened with a spit!

Your proud grace and perfect dignity of bearing
Are such poetry in motion to the eye.
And your leaps embued with breathless levitation
Make the corps de ballet enviously sigh.

So fastidious you are about your grooming,
Washing frequently your handsome whiskered face,
Making absolutely sure that you've manicured each paw
And there's not a single hair that's out of place.

You'll forgive me if in fondness and affection
I do place a kiss upon you silky head.
As I stroke your velvet paw, you'll subdue a gentle snore -
Yawn politely, and discretely make for bed!

Pauline Hight

RESPECT FOR ANIMALS

Respect for animals is what we need,
So people stop using them for feed,
There is no need for this as science will show,
People don't need meat to grow.

Their short life they live alone,
No-one to comfort them in the murder zone.
Respect for animals is what we need,
So please stop using them to feed.

Respect for animals!

Helen Hurst

DOG

We put an expensive collar
on our dog's neck,
we give him best dog food
for his daily bread.
We love him dearly
and cry at his death,
but do we ever wonder
at the meaning
of the howling and screaming
coming over him sometimes.
What is this longing,
this silent torture of the heart
which makes him do that?

Maybe he cries
for not being given the choice
between harsh freedom of nature
and coy enslavement of human love.

Jolanta Grynkiewicz

CRY OF THE WHALE

All alone in this huge place,
Whale I heard your song.
Lonely cries of hurt and pain,
Separated from mum.
Who was slaughtered by the Japanese
Your death was soon to come
Nowhere to run,
Nowhere to hide,
From this tragedy which is no longer fun
All alone in this huge place,
Whale I heard your song.

Claire Marden

ANGEL AND FRIEND

Bewildered, so cold and so hungry,
He didn't know which way to go.
How could they leave him, battered and bruised,
When he had loved them, so?

His body ached, he longed for sleep;
Tiny feet, torn and so sore.
Too weary, even to whimper;
He couldn't go on any more.

'What happened to you, my little one,
Who did this to you, little pup?'
An angel had found him, just in time,
Gentle hands were lifting him up.

She held him close and warmed him;
Swift footsteps carried him home.
Somehow, he knew this angel would love him,
Something told him he wasn't alone.

Slowly, but surely, Angel nursed him,
Until, at last, he was well.
Soft, brown eyes spoke his gratitude,
Much more than words could tell.

For Angel and Friend, there's no parting;
Both have found love and trust.
All memories of pain and hopelessness,
Have crumbled and turned to dust.

Janet Swindells

THE ELEPHANT

Eyes like toffee, soft and creamy,
Yet filled with anxiety.
The mother elephant nudges her dead baby,
Wondering why he won't wake up.

She rolls him over and kneels down beside him
Her strong trunk draped lovingly
Across his back.
His small body lies motionless -

On the dry dusty ground,
Peaceful and quiet
The mother leans against him,
Her head on his.

Then she nudges him again,
More desperately this time,
As if trying to will life into his little soul.
Her great ears flap gently,

Swotting the flies buzzing round her head.
But not even these small creatures
Are afraid of the elephant.
This strong and powerful being
Shows no sign of her intelligent unease.
She appears calm.
Her placid brown eyes provoke no fear in the insects
They believe that she is content as she is,

Lying next to her little one,
Protective and immense
Eventually, she cradles him up in her great trunk
And carries on with her search

For her herd.
After many hours of roaming,
She sets him softly down on the dry earth
And wanders alone.

Clare Aldridge (12)

WHISKEY AND FRED

A lonely bush
planted with care.
A resting place
for Whiskey and Fred.

You sleep beneath
its sheltering leaves.
Yellow and green
a sight to be seen.

How we still miss you
Whiskey, black and white.
Fred, your coat was like snow
a wondrous sight.

We will never forget you
the bush will remind us.
Through winter and summer
its leaves remain.

No one can replace you,
as the years roll by.
One day we'll meet again
in a happy place.

Thora Carpenter

THE HUNTSMAN

A graceful elegance
A life shortly begun,
Which is impetuously ended
By an ignorant man with a gun.
Greed reflects in his eyes
He displays no shame,
But an animal is dead
and he's to blame.
He's got what he wanted
The impassive fool!
No realisation he's been careless
and cruel.
With no thought to its family
Which is now minus one,
An animal once breathing
now wrongfully gone.
He collects his reward
And leaves behind much pain,
As he walks away contented
The huntsman strikes . . . again.

Joanne Timmins (17)

THE DEATH OF A FOX

His home was the silver woods,
Roaming free by the lakes by the trees,
With shyness he hides from life.

One day the hunt rode by,
The sparkling sun reflected his ginger coat,
By the lakes by the trees,
he was seen by his home,
Deep under those trees.

Hideous hounds have made their sounds,
The fox lays dead,
By his lake by the trees.

All the trees cried out in triumphant song,
For the fox that once roamed free,
By the lake by the trees.

James Stewart

THE GUARD DOG

Pity the poor dog that the owner kicks,
The one that slinks into the corner,
Why did he deserve such treatment,
From a master who thinks the dog doesn't feel
The kick that connected with his heel.
Hoping the dog will respond to his command,
when he tells him to sit.

When the night is cold and dark,
And the dog in the corner begins to bark
The owner runs down to find a thief,
Just about to run off with a hundred quid,
After the thief is apprehended,
The dog gets a bone and a pat on the head
He takes it off to eat in his bed.

When the house is in darkness again,
The dog remembers the intense pain,
Hoping his owner has decided to quit,
He curls in a ball and goes back to sleep
Licking his lips to remember the taste
Of the bone that he got from the master he hates.

Jacqueline Bentley

AFRICAN ANIMALS

Elephants majestically stride
  Lions timidly hide, with young cubs to guide
  Giraffes glide, across the plains
Fleeting swiftly, passed again
  Beautiful spotted cheetah
  Proudly sits serene
  Midst branches, of leafy green
Sun rises high in the African sky
  Glorious birds, go flying by
Rhinos pass, quietly on
  Stalking, and are gone
Sun leaves, a shimmering haze
  For long hot, sultry days
  The sunset's red, adds a fiery touch
  As day, turns into dusk
  Safari camp fires, begin to burn
Dusk to darkness, once more turns.

Irene G Corbett

WEARING FURS

We must respect the animals,
We cannot kill them for their fur.
Did 'my lady' really need that coat?
Or was it just another whim.
There are plenty of imitations,
That would keep you just as warm.
Let the animals, live their lives,
In dignity, without harm.
No need for brutal cruelty,
Killing them, just to get their skin.
Try giving, a little kindness,
Wearing furs, is wearing thin.

Shirley Thompson

BEFRIENDED

He beat his dog
constantly daily
it became ordinary accepted
the dog expected
abuse.
The man
became an automatic brainless robot
beating, kicking cursing
he didn't care
until -
his neighbour
twice his size
twice as frightening
beat kicked and cursed him
on the dog's behalf.

Kathleen Bradley

FOR US TO YOU

We're sheep and calves exported to hell,
Please good people, our stories do tell.
We're tiny cute chicks, cramped, plucked and hung.
Demand us free range, and then we've won.
We're elephants, for our ivory they kill,
Let's go for the stampede, no tusks to steal.
We're rabbits, stewed or made to measure,
Cuddle me rather, I'm yours to treasure,
We're seal cubs so cute, and white as snow,
Just leave us alone, our numbers won't grow.
We're animals, you're humans, but it gives you no right,
To abuse us for greed, when money's in sight.
We don't ask for much, this plea don't reject.
What we need from all humans, is love and respect.

Jill Oleszko

SKIN DEEP

'tis amazing,' roared the tiger,
'that they want to wear my skin!'
'Handbags!' moaned the alligator.
'They want mine to put things in!'

'They look on me as just a rug . . .
for them to warm their feet!'
'twas clear the bear was grizzly, so . . .
they quickly took a seat.

The tiger winked: 'Let's try to help!'
'But, why?' they both replied.
'Don't you two feel a certain need,
below . . . deep down inside?'

'Yes-yes!' they cried. 'Do please explain?'
'Just wait . . . and when you see
the next three humans passing by . . .
we'll 'ave 'em for our tea!'

'But how will that help them?' they asked.
The tiger gave a grin.
'Down there, it's warm . . . with room for things . . .
and . . . each can wear a skin!'

Bryan Moore

A WHALE FOR THE KILLING

A whale for the killing, so let's have some sport,
For great fun such as this surely cannot be bought.
Some say it's the last and it could well be true,
For it's many years past that they killed the last few.

Don't let it escape - what a tragedy then -
That the last of a species should live out its span.
Kill! Kill! Comes the cry, strike at all that has life,
For we've crushed and we've mangled, now let murder run rife.

Men have toiled down the years to perfecting their skill,
They have put all their brainpower into how best to kill;
And slowly at first, till perfection attained,
God's creatures were massacred, their blood the earth stained.

There are some who recall, though it's hard to believe,
When with fishes of beauty the sea boiled and heaved;
And the land and the air with wild creatures was blessed,
But they've gone to men's greed, and his wars did the rest.

Pat Hubbard

TO A STRAY CAT

Was it our need for you
Or your need for us that brought us together?
A mutual desire to comfort and be comforted;
A friendship and trust forged from the mirrored experiences
Of want and being wanted.
Or is your loyalty no deeper than the bowl of scraps
That first lured you to our door,
And ours as fickle as the falling rain
That gently swelled the springtime buds,
Then cruelly bruised the ripening autumn grain?

You come and go - no prison cell our home;
Here welcome you will always be;
But should your former life, or loved ones dear
Return to call you back,
Move on, sweet creature of the night,
Remain forever free;
Yet stay with us to haunt our lives with perfect charity.

Heather N Collister

THE PACK
(for Bonny)

Their eyes are moon
Flecked and ever
Awake, amber sentinels,
Watching, unblinking,
And scenting, hunting, sniffing
Out fear and prey.
They live out beyond, bolting
Between snows and frosted skies
Their howls wavering for miles
Amongst the midnight mists.
Then pack trailing, silently
Skating the iced lakes, smoothly
And quietly as pawless ghosts,
Leaving a lone well padded track,
Mark of passing;
In-between dangers,
Necessity, and man's misunderstanding
Myths and symbol wraiths that choke
Needlessly, territories, forests
And their night.
Feared for a freedom
We have forever forgotten;
Mistrustful and trapped between
Respect and prejudice, they survive,
Somehow living, self concealed,
And always running,
Calling softly
From a snow cragged
Mountain edge.

Jenny Middleton

WHY?

Why do you treat me the way you do,
causing me pain in all sorts of ways?
Keeping me cooped up in a cell behind bars
to be gawped at, and pointed at every day.
Why do you chain me, and put rings through my nose,
make me walk on hot plates and force me to 'dance'?
Hunting me down, just for your sport
and cheating me out of my very existence.

Why do you do this? I do you no harm.

And why do you make me dependent on you,
and then starve me, or beat me? It's not fair.
If you do not want me, then why do you keep me,
instead of giving me to those who care?
Why, when I've done nothing to hurt you,
do you keep me confined in tiny places,
sticking needles all over my body,
and giving me all sorts of terrible diseases?

Why do you do this? I mean you no ill.

And why are you cutting down the forests?
You know you are destroying my home.
And what for? To make more and more burgers,
or to build more and more homes of your own.
Why is it that you are cutting me down,
or shooting me, or bashing my head?
Just so you can make different things from my body -
souvenirs of the dead.

I'm only trying to live the way that nature intends,
so why do you treat me this way? I don't understand.

Conny Armstrong

125

RESPECT FOR ANIMALS

Again, I am driven to write about animals;
they need respect and rights
but do not have them.
Animals are completely under our control,
they cannot fight for themselves
and do not bear malice to anyone.
How people can wear furs and fur coats
I do not know,
because the animal who wore it last
died in it.
I do wish people would think this way;
there are plenty of artificial clothes
people can wear
and to make wool sheep have their coats
sheared to cool them down.
So why do we have to use skins
and the suffering that animals come through;
it is abominable and makes me feel
the pain that they must suffer
but people seem to be becoming more
and more cruel,
against themselves as well.
How can it be that there is so much
suffering and heartache.
Animals kill for food and to keep
themselves alive
and it is outright, no pain and feeling
is attached.
So why can we not have more
respect for animals.

Irene Elliot

A PROTESTER'S GLIMPSE OF A VEAL CALF

Only a metal bar, a cold, hard, metal bar
for you to suck and to seek comfort from
does not give you the nourishment you crave
or help quench your thirst, nor give you any comfort.
The people who threw you onto that lorry
are like that bar of steel
cold, hard, unyielding.
Your mother was soft
she gave you comfort, food and shelter
she loved you and cared for you
like most mothers do for their babies.
She cried for days when the man who looked after her
took you away from her
and prevented her from joining you on the lorry.
You peer out at us, curiosity on your face
as if you wonder where you are going
as if this journey may be taking you to some exciting place
as if you wonder what life has in store for you.
Soon you will find out.
This is your last day of daylight
you will never see green fields again
your destination is a wooden coffin
a slatted floor, unsuitable for your little hoofs
your muscles will not grow,
your digestive system will not develop
your flesh will remain the palest of pink, to satisfy those,
whose only interest in you is that pale flesh.
When the time comes for you to leave your coffin
too weak to walk, you will be carried
to your place of execution.

Lilian Taylor

A WOLF CRIES

A male wolf sits beneath the moon, with muted voice, he cries.
He cries about the world of man, man's cruelty, and lies.
He cries for his shrinking forests,
And for his poisoned streams;
For the pain caused by the wolf traps
That haunt his lonely dreams.
He cries because his pack mates
Are afraid, and on the run
From the only predator they fear,
A scared man with a gun.
He cries for all the other wolves
So cruelly hunted down,
Because a little human child
Is missing from his town.
He cries for the misty mountains,
And the forests of his home.
Where will all the wolves go
When there's no room left to roam?
He cries for his ever-changing world,
And for a life he used to know
Before man came with his prejudice.
Ah but that was long ago.
He cries for all those sacrificed
In vanity's harsh name
To provide wolf fur coats for women
Who parade them without shame.
He raises an age-grey muzzle
In mute reverence to the sky.
Then, in the eerie glow of moonlight
He lets out another cry.

J Lingard

CREATURES OF EARTH

If you were born an animal,
How would you like to be,
Brought into this lovely world,
Yet it, you never see,
Locked in batteries, pens and sheds,
Fed and watered too,
Never seeing light of day,
For some animals, this is true,
Fattened up, then taken,
To be killed for human greed,
Slaughtered, and your babies torn,
From their mums, that they still need,
Seal culls, killing baby seals,
Their mums' hearts just to break,
Why is this so needed,
I think for pity's sake,
That all those things, should stop right now,
Put yourself in their place,
Would you like it done to you,
I don't think I could face,
This world, or life within it,
If that was meant for me,
I'd want to stay in spirit world,
And not come here, you see,
God made us all as beings,
Of love and light and peace,
Not only us, as humans,
But what we sow, we'll reap.

Janette Campbell

THE GREAT NEED FOR RESPECT

Have you ever seen on your TV screen
Giant gorillas
Cuddling and loving their young?
The intelligence in their eyes
Worldly wise.
Elephants moving timber,
Orders rarely needed,
Knowing exactly what to do?
Cattle going to slaughter . .
Do you think they don't know?
I shrink from the wondering fear
In their beautiful eyes.
Sheep too, poor scared creatures,
Suffocatingly packed in their dreadful tumbrels.
Woolly they may be, but not woolly-headed,
They know.
They all breathe the air we breathe,
Feel pleasure, pain and fear
As do you and I.
But man's cruelty and greed
Decreed, one thing they would not share,
To live a normal lifespan
As do you and I.
So much hidden suffering
Throughout the world is there,
Thank God for all those people
Who act, and really care,
And knowing of their many plights
Fight, unrewarded, for animal rights.

Irene Locke

THE FOXES OF GIPSY HILL

Walking slowly, down to Gipsy Hill,
the air is warm and sultry still and scented
with the thrill of summer jasmine.
In the Colby Arms, ice cold stout,
Backgammon and trivial conversation,
'til it's time to chuck us out.

Back up the hill, I notice the arabis
pouring forth, like stout,
its creamy white head of froth
over crumbling garden walls.
Sometimes,
very late, about this time of year,
I hear the lonely calls of the nightingale.

In the pale orange light,
two young foxes have come out to play.
They romp and fight a way up the street,
but make no sound with their intimate mouths,
or their softly padded feet.

The moon hangs, low and limpid
in the London glow of a humid sky
like a distant, misty gem.
The foxes are peering down the hill
and they've noticed me . . . notice them.

For a moment they look
. . . and listen,
standing in line, so very near
. . . stock still.
Then, suddenly they move,
passing me close without a sign of fear
. . . walking slowly, down to Gipsy Hill.

John Merritt

THE DEAD FOX BY THE MOTORWAY

A beautiful red-gold bundle
Lay dead beside the road.

We drive our tar and stone
Across the fox's land.
He trots out to explore
And is suddenly no more.
No more than a lonely bundle
Of sad brown fur.

I passed a lorry full
Of dark green pines
Destined to die indoors
A glorious death with tinsel.
The soft fir arms waved at me
'Help!' they cried, 'help!
This morning we were upright
Quietly in the earth.
Now this mad dash
Mad ride to starry doom.'

Their cry was lost in the rush of air
Heard only by me and the hawk
Silently hovering there.

Charmian Goldwyn

REVERSE THE ACTION

Cries and fears fill the fields,
    As the huntsmen ride and scout

People cover their eyes, agree it's foul,
    But cries still shout

Poor fox, it has no help at all,
    The ground has nowhere for it to crawl

It's hopeless for one so small,
      Being tortured by those 'great lords'

Let's reverse the action and see
      If they would like to be hunted
      And tormented with no humanity at all

M E Fuller

FUR OF PUREST WHITE

Come, see the bear, majestic, fur of purest white,
Pacing the pit from dawn until night,
Four and twenty paces left, then four and twenty right.

With Ray, young Philip, Louise and Haz,
At Dudley zoo on Easter holidays,
I saw a sight my mind just can't erase.
A creature from cold lands of ice and snow,
Imprisoned, just for public show,
Frustrated in his boredom, spirits low.

Come, see the bear, majestic, fur of purest white,
Pacing the pit from dawn until night,
Four and twenty paces left, then four and twenty right.

From Canada, or some far distant land,
Created by God's gentle, loving hand,
From his natural home so sad and cruelly banned.
Did God create such beauty for a cage,
To perform for man upon this gloomy stage?
Dear God, forgive mankind for such outrage!

Come, see the bear, majestic, fur of purest white,
Pacing the pit from dawn until night,
Four and twenty paces left, then four and twenty right.

Mike Smith

DUMB AND BEAUTIFUL

Be it a feline a dog a mouse or a rat
Each and every animal is God's creature and that's that.
Every animal deserves the right to live, they can be
Fun loving and full of pleasure to give.
Myself I am a pet owner two dogs I have with me.
They're small and friendly and very cuddly.
To learn of an animal that's been mistreated is beyond
A fact of life for, they cannot put up a fight
or defend themselves with a weapon such as a knife.
My heart goes out to all pet lovers for they
deserve to own a pet.
For if you give them love, in return pleasure
you will get.
And to all animal hospitals, rescue homes and such,
They cater for the neglected and give loving care much.
Give a pet a loving caring home in which they'll
be glad to stay.
For a pet is not just for five minutes, it's for
each and every day.

Trevor Barnes

WOUNDED BIRD

The bird I held in tender cupped hand fold
as it gazed up with eyes in frightened plea,
Too weak to take to flight in jaunting bold
it had to helpless rest in crumpled scree.

I smoothed it gentle as I fed in drop
the smallest morsel which it swallowed whole,
Then it balled there with patient trust to stop
content to let me suffer for its soul.

When strong enough I aided its escape
and watched as with a joyful song it flew,
To bring a tear at the spectre in free drape
as my feathered friend swung in flighted dew.

I could not forget the look from its eyes
as I nursed it with love in ambience filled,
With care for creatures in all forms and size
that are part of the grand design God willed.

Aileen Hopkins

THE RIDING LESSON!

'Now put you feet in the stirrups'
'Hold the reins lightly and firmly'
'You must let the horse know you are there'
Thus began the first riding lesson!
In this field so green, with a wide path
They all set off, round and round.
'All stop still' called the teacher.
But how did she stop this creature who had a mind of his own?
'Whoa, whoa' she called, but it fell on deaf ears,
Then gradually he slowed and stopped.
'Now we will do some trotting, so get your horse moving'
But her horse still walked sedately along.
First she dug her heels in and nothing happened,
So then she tried her toes. 'What next?' she thought,
'Do it harder' the teacher called
Then all of a sudden they were *off!*
But why was she going down when it should be up?
Soon it was the end of the first riding lesson.
Would she ever walk again?
Of all God's creatures the horse is best!

Margaret Pearce

FOOD FOR THOUGHT

Trap it,
Skin it,
Make it bleed -
Hunt it,
Shoot it,
Take its seed -
Pet it,
Vet it,
Sanction its need -
Stud it,
Snip it,
Evaluate the breed -

Synthesise and sterilise,
And serve as chicken feed.

David Hicks

QUEST

Our quest, to stop the agony
Of animals sent over sea
In summer storm, in winter gale,
Vulnerable, afraid and frail.
Animals whose dreadful fate
Finds them trapped in dark, cramped crate
Before their end. They have no choice.
They have no rights, they have no voice.
This trade goes on. We *must* keep trying
To change the rules of where they're dying,
These heaving, gasping calves and sheep.
Here must be their final sleep.

Harness our power! Ahead there may be glory -
A happy ending to this shameful story.

Elizabeth Mark

136

YOUNG ALFIE

Galloping hooves
across a field
he is our shield,
racehorse breed
no doubt he is,
long fawn limbs
brown tossed mane
chasing away doubts,
gathering momentum
in his bliss
at being at one
with long green grass
and racing clouds
he is built for this.
He nods at birds
no need for words,
the imprint of his hooves,
he gallops again
into our hearts
and in the main
responds to trust.
The stable door
is open wide
his master's ride
his joy and pride.

Joan Hands

ELEPHANT'S TEARS

The music plays
The elephant sways
Unsteady in the spotlight.
Tawdry sequins sparkle
Reflect tears, in the elephant's eyes.

Turning slowly
He pirouettes
The elephant *never* forgets,
As he bows and he prances
Spins and he dances,
He can beg
But he will *never* be free.

The elephant turns
The harness burns
Like tears, in the elephant's eyes,
His cries are lost
In the roar of the crowd
Who laugh,
At the elephant's tears.

Jacqueline

NOT A CHANCE

Over fields and hills,
The hounds run in packs,
The horses gallop
Huntsmen on their backs

Chasing a fox
They call it sport
To beat and rip it up
They should be taken to court

The fox races desperately
Not looking back to glance
Tries clinging on for life
It hasn't got a chance

The fox has to surrender
He was doomed from the start
And all for some fun
On the huntsmen's part

Lorna Mitchell (15)

IN A LAB FOR LIFE

Nice teeth, the toothpaste was
tested on 8000 cats.
I got angry with fluffy, sweet
thing, gave him to Cat Protection
League.
You know beagles, kept in cages -
made to smoke cigarettes.
We already know they cause heart
disease, it's lucrative.

TV shows little, the adverts
are worse than lies.
If all animal lovers protested,
vivisection might end.

Monkeys get operated on while
still conscious, they only know fear,
you want to eradicate disease, no
hope unless we're robots.

A world of robots, animals screaming
in their billions, scientists laughing
in pubs and patting dogs on the head.

Paul Desca

THE BADGER

Man has hunted and trapped badgers for their hair
More are killed on the road than anywhere
Some take part in dog baiting an horrendous sport
It's illegal and these men should be caught
Badgers favourite food is the earthworm
When will these men learn.
The badger's home is an underground sett
I think they'd make a nice pet.
The badger is a true omnivore.
They forage for ten hours or more.
Eating slugs, plants, frogs and moles
Also rabbits, fruits, rats and voles.
They have an acute sense of smell
And good hearing as well
Although their eyesight is poor
They're usually found in woods, hedges and moor
From February to March they usually mate
In cold weather they do not hibernate
Man must stop causing them undue stress
Stop hunting them or perhaps less.

Kay Brown

DETER THE KILLING

In this the twentieth century, we should deter
The killing and suffering, in supplying real fur
Imitations look grand upon human backs
But why, oh why, must there be cruel traps

Fashion designers can make their wealth
Glamorous fabrics, instead of fur pelts
The status of owning a real mink coat
Think of the animal instead of yourself

To exploit God's creatures, does not make sense
Aimed at the helpless animals' expense
For some, saving animals is a worthy cause
For others, indifference to the suffering they cause.

Rita Humphrey

ANIMALS' PAIN, A HUMAN'S GAIN

Do you think this is right?
Do you think this is usual?
Do you think it doesn't matter
Because they can't speak?
Do you think they won't mind
To be abused,
Locked in cages,
For you to stare and laugh at?
As though their existence
Is meant for you.
You make me angry
You wouldn't want this
For any human
You cry when your friends are hurt
And when someone you love dies.
Why is it different for an animal?
They breathe,
They can feel pain
And they know when they are dying
And you still hurt them.
There is something wrong
With the human race.

Carrol C Lawless

FOX

The watcher waits
in the darkness
Tense and stiffened by
early morning cold
He has been here for
hours in anticipation.

The first glow of dawn
a redness on the horizon
Will the prey come before daylight
No it's just another wasted night
of hunger and desperation

As the golden shafts of
sunlight tear through vegetation
Like a thief he slinks
back to his accommodation.

Gavin Queen

THE CAT

A butterfly flirted with the sun
Its kaleidoscopic colours almost iridescent
As it fluttered without a care.
The cat watched, mesmerised
As this beauty was flaunted before her.
Her muscles tensed involuntarily
And her tail lashed without control.
Suddenly, jealous of it, she sprang
And batted the butterfly with a fistful of claws.
It fell at once, wings torn, its flying days over.
The cat looked at the dead butterfly
And yowled in tortured anguish.
She felt as if she had destroyed her own soul.

Helen Ireson

TIMIDITY

Mouse, as an element of landscape,
Unusual: a crackle in the hedge
Becomes bold by starlight,
Hesitates,
Takes stock of autumn
Then leads her scampering brood -
Handfuls past Heaven -
Foraging Fierce and Fearless into the wood.
I dare at last to breathe.
The terrible marauders passed me by
As scarcely worth a bite.

Indoors, another matter. Winter's night
Draws him across the stone. My monolith
Lets fall a careless crumb, another one . . .
I fall into his trap and find it fun.

Alasdair Aston

THE ANIMAL WORLD . . .

All the animals in the world are treated really bad
when I see them on TV it makes me really sad,
Animals being tested on is really just not fair,
All they really need is just some love and care,
Rabbits being tested on, mice being used
and all the other animals which are being abused,
I think its really disgusting. The way that people talk
as if any other animal has no right to live or walk,
They all have thoughts and feelings, just like me or you
except they have no choice when someone says their life is through,
So if anyone wants to help them then listen to what I say
all the animals need our help not tomorrow but today.

Wendy Oldrey

THE RABBIT

It was just a baby rabbit
Nibbling clover on the lawn
Then cleaning up its whiskers
It really looked so cute

But when it was discovered
Cabbage plants were all chewed off
Though seeming sweet, that rabbit
Must be given the boot

We shoo'd it out the first time
Plugging every single gap
Still it was back next morning
By another route

More barricades were put up
Wiring, netting all fresh plants
But that bunny ate the lot
Caring not a hoot!

Each day we never found it
After chases round the lawn
It vanished from the fruit trees
To where it would scoot

It grew a long-legged teenager
Started bringing in its pals
We got them out, but number one
Never followed suit

Yet strange to say, I've missed it
Since one day it disappeared
I hope no-one made that bunny
A target to shoot.

Dorothy Dosson

SPEED KING

Strangest of felines
narrow bodied
standing high off the ground
long tail, spotted
contradictory
voice lacking a roar
claws non retractable
diurnal, purring cat
huntsman by day
eyesight keen
surveying the open savannah
languishing
crouched upon a hillock, watching
no need to rely on surprise
overcome your antelope prey
running them down
outstripping
every other earthly animal
speed your essence
lacking in endurance
sprawl exhausted
after the heat of the chase
hide your hard earned kill
from unwanted attention

Chris Birkitt

DO THEY?

When the lion hunts and
Stalks his prey
Does he think this kill
Will feed us today
When turtles scurry down
To the sea
Know the ocean is a safe
Place to be,
Ants working hard to move
The soil,
Know they are helping
With their toil,
And my cat when she sits
And stares at the wall
Does she think of anything
At all,
Do the cattle and sheep
Know it's a one-way ride
As they look through the
Slats of the packed lorries
Side,
That they won't smell or see
The green fields again,
Are they frightened do
They feel the pain?

Patsy Sharpe

AFTER CATULLUS: VICTORIA

After Catullus, what can one say?
Perhaps that she whom I love best
Does indeed soothe my brooding pain
And heavy passions drowse again.
My darling, darling Victoria:
Do not die;
I simply could not bear it.
Especially if I thought I was to blame.
There is no Latin word for grass
Parakeet or budgie;
But could any sparrow of Catullus
Who could play and ease
His anxious love away,
Be more adorable, pretty?
I love her more than any baby
Or even any child.
Except perhaps one:
Not, indeed, my own,
And why I do not know or cannot say.
I saw him:
A little, poor kid in a woolly cardigan.
I had met a friend for coffee
But quickly left to shop:
Thus nearly collided into him;
But stopped myself and gently touched him,
As might some avenging angel,
Binding the power of its mighty wings:
And, as I did so,
Unaccountably, a terrible, blinding pain
Shot through my tormented heart.

J Skinner

INTENSIVE HOLOCAUST

I long to be proud of what and who I am, my very own species
Yet not a day passes by without a solemn, guilty thought
A melancholy echo, dancing circles within my mind;
The many books, the many pictures . . . I study far too intensely -
Ashamed, embarrassed; the wonderful possibility of a peaceful, ethical world
Again washes over me, entirely spoiled, tarnished
Like a dark shroud, shielding the pale, ivory moon.

Deep, saddened, bewildered eyes of the motherless calf,
I long to cup your dear, trusting face in my loving palms
And to smooth your matted skin, ease your fretful mind.
Yet how can I do so when you are enclosed, imprisoned behind torturous
                                              bars?
Hard, slatted flooring, no room for movement or growth
No fresh smelling straw to rest your weary head,
No water to lap deliciously, from sheer neglected thirst . . .
I so much long to free your pained, helpless body
To watch you skip delightfully through buttercup fields,
And nuzzle angelically, as you drink the milk from your mother
That is so rightfully yours, not ours.
Your lifeless body, your cruel, shortened time on this planet
Will mean little to the brutal, burly farmer, who shall cart you away
With hundreds just like you . . . under-nourished, over-produced,
All so pitifully pining, cramped in horrendous conditions, too weak to object.
Next stop is the slaughterhouse, many miles away . . .
One huge, blooded production-line, treated no better than a cardboard box,
Pushed, shoved maliciously, bruising you, whipping you . . your precious
                                              body suffers.
Nobody to comfort you or take the pain away . . your pleading, deep eyes
                                    will forever haunt me.

A better life must surely await you, I pray fervently.
I sigh, overwhelmed with grief, and wait patiently at the docks,
Anticipating the next lorry load, which I hear thundering along the worn
road,
This time, further horror awaits me, as the docile, haunting glare of sheep
greets me . . .

Melanie Growden

THE BEAR

We never lingered in our bed
If mum and dad said Heysham Head
lots of amusements and a zoo
all were there for me and you

We ran to see the bear in the pit
It always knew us I'm sure of it
Only now as I think of its plight
Stuck in that hole it just wasn't right

It had no friends it had no say
down that hole it had to stay
I feel so sad as I think of it now
It had to stick it I don't know how

Animals can always been seen on TV
No need to cage them they should be free
After all would we like their life?
I know I wouldn't and that is my gripe

Alas Heysham Head amusements are gone
concerts and swingboats there are none
No more tea and cakes in the cafe
Now it's just a dot on the map.

Francine L

GOODBYE CRUEL WORLD

She looked down on her calf just born
her heart her soul they were torn
Sorry son you're bred for meat
he took me away from my mother's teat
her anguished soul cried out in pain
Bring my son back again
He laughed and smirked he's mine too
Tears now welling in his eyes
Can't see his mum but hears her cries
A long journey he had to endure
On board a ship for a day or two
Took me away from my mother's breast
Put me in a crate to look my best
For fattening is the thing they do
Six months of this I have to endure
To make me nice and white for veal
So you can have a tasty meal.

S Carr

FASHION VICTIM

Hey Miss Sable wanna wear my coat?
It's thin and pink and it's mine for you.
It won't do you any good,
It won't look as good on me as you
but Elle and Vogue all want you to.
You know they're right, they always are.
They tell you what's hip, what's cool.
You read; you follow,
go on wear my coat, you know you will.

She'd never take the coat off my back,
she's happy with what she has.
It isn't fashion, it isn't cool, it's hers.
Her boyfriend still loves her; he thinks she's cute.
She doesn't want to be a model
On the cover of a magazine.
She wants to go home tonight, where she's warm,
She wants to take her coat home from the club.
It's where they belong; together.

Vickie Simpson

ANIMALS

Animals are forever,
just like you and me.
People say it's great to kill,
it's the same as killing me.
How would you feel being
exported or put into a ring?
Animals do have feelings,
help them and join in.

By the time we get to 50
there'll only be you and me.
Our kids will only see pictures
of what there used to be.

So come on give it a try
there's only once chance you'll get.
Let's all join together and unite
and never try to forget.

Kelly Porter

DEAR LORD, ACCEPT THE PRAYERS WE OFFER
(A hymn for all creatures)

Dear Lord, accept the prayers we offer,
For all Thy creatures in our care.
That none may suffer fear or violence,
Your guiding hand be always there.

For each and every humble sparrow,
Our Master marks their single fall.
Teach us to strive, and never weaken
The tireless fight to save them all.

Give us a heart of tender mercy,
Let no wild beast in suffering lie.
For them eternal freedom granted,
By hunters gun no more shall die.

Far round the world this prayer is offered
For strength and guidance from above,
Make us aware of all their suffering,
And keep them in Your wondrous love.

Linda J Bodicoat

BECOMING A VEGGIE!

What are we doing to these poor animals,
If you think about it we are really cannibals,
That pork chop you ate was once a playful piglet,
Would you not rather have a tasty Twiglet?

Beef, pork, lamb and chicken are probably most of your favourite meals,
Not to mention those fish who are brought in on painful reels,
Next time you eat a piece of animal flesh,
Think of them being transported and banging against mesh.

Think of them getting tortured then killed,
I bet the butchers are really thrilled,
So if you want to put an end to this
Then give meat eating a big *miss*

So what if your parents become edgy
When you decide to become a veggie!

Sarah Wilson (15)

JOURNEY TO THE SLAUGHTERHOUSE

You have eyes yet do not see,
The cruelty and pain inflicted on us,
As you pull, push,
Crate and cram us,
Into horrible, crowded lorries.
You have ears yet do not hear,
As we shout and squall,
Scream and bawl,
In an effort to overcome our fears.
You have hands which do o good deed
As you haul, hurl,
Harm and hurt us,
Nothing you do, can heal or calm us.
You have mouths yet do not speak.
One word of comfort
As we stand and stare
On the floor so bare,
None of you seem to really care.
Hunger, thirst and fatigue,
Is our life until finally ended,
A journey so cruel and barbaric,
A practice that must be amended.

Catherine Hasler

A DAY IN THE LIFE OF

'Vic' the vivisectionist,
Sets about his daily chores,
Injecting mice with oven cleaner,
And measuring their sores.

'This test was most enlightening,'
He writes in his report,
'These tiny mice, took hours to die,
Much longer than was thought.

Internal bleeding and convulsions,
Their faces contorted with pain,
So astonished by the result,
I ran the test again and again.

In finding a poison to torture mice,
I've certainly succeeded,
Though the product itself, is not ready for the shelf;
More research here is needed.

'A new batch of subjects,' he thinks to himself,
As he grabs the ill-fated rat.
'Incompatible to us, but what's all the fuss?
No-one need ever know that!'

A frustrated physician, 'a man on a mission',
Initiates his incision.
No anaesthetic, the cries are pathetic,
Refusal of any remission.

Blood-stained lab coat,
A murderous shroud,
The attire of a tyrant,
Of which you are proud.

Your actions have been witnessed,
Your debt must be collected,
Revenge enforced, your soul endorsed,
To be eternally dissected.

R Jordan

CARING

God made the world a lovely place, with
everything we need. The sky, sand and sea, the birds,
fields and trees.

Then he made a perfect man, with something
called free-will; and filled the sea with shoals of fish
and animals in fields. He added birds and creatures and
flowers to smell and see.

He even made this man a wife - so beautiful
to see.

Soon the devil crept along and quickly changed
the man. He now is hard and full of greed, cares
not for right or wrong. He's ruining our planet,
killing birds and wildlife too. As if that is not
bad enough, he makes them suffer too.

We must end the suffering of creatures great
and small by spreading the word to all we meet
and get them to do it too.

I know God in heaven must be shedding
many tears, to find he couldn't trust us for even
a few years.

He has promised in the Bible He is coming back
again to end this world and take a few of us to heaven
who *respect* and love His name.

Julie Holmes

WITH RESPECT

Our earth's creatures great or small,
Should we not respect them *all?*
Somewhere, along life's way,
Has true compassion not - *gone astray*?

We loudly *voice* our love, and care,
Buy pets galore to stroke, to share.
Yet, on our plates with knife and fork
Dismember flesh, and never balk.

This animal life we use as prey
For ourselves, our pets, yes, every day.
Yet, earth provides much *other* food,
Nutritious, varied, healthy, good.

I ask you, do not turn away -
From unsettling thought, traditional sway.
Think on the 'sentient creatures' we breed,
Those we *use, abuse,* then *bleed.*

Their plight should lie heavy on *every* heart,
Their uncalled for death, *tear us,* apart.
Life has provided *alternative fayre,*
Let compassion *rule, 'really care'.*

This theme has wider aspects, too,
Of mother earth, of me, and you.
Blood letting ways cause fear, cause ill -
Reflections dark, on nature's plan
Not just for beast, but upon you, *man.*

As you pray for your peace, in every way,
Give the word peace, *total* play.
Give, the bell of peace, a worldwide ring,
For *planet, beast, man, - everything.*

D Glossop

PURRFECT LANDING

Charlie is my kitten as black as black could be,
Her two green eyes at night-time are all that you can see.
She plays all day with anything, a butterfly, the rain,
Until it's time for dinner, then she appears again.

Millie is her mother, black, save for face and feet,
As large and powerful a cat as you would wish to meet.
One day a friendly dog called Ben, came to stay for tea,
He teamed with our dog Bella and chased cats from my knee.

Charlie raced out of the house the dogs in hot pursuit,
I tried to stop them oh so hard, but they jumped o'er my boot.
Now Millie got protective and turned to face the foe,
The dogs amazed both stood quite still, expecting her to go.

As smiles merged into large white teeth, Millie had a fright,
She scrambled up the curtains till nearly out of sight.
It would have been quite safe up there, if the curtains had not ripped,
Our Millie lost her footing, as claws gave way, she slipped.

Sent flying through the air towards those gaping jaws,
Her face was full of horror as she spread out all her claws.
She landed firmly on Ben's head, he yelped as claws stuck in,
I could not help but notice that Millie wore a grin.

As her claws sank ever deeper, the dogs retreated fast,
Millie let out one more hiss, released her claws at last.
Now from that day each movement, is treated as suspect,
Both dogs and cats are wary, it must be called respect.

Russell Thorndale

UNTITLED

He's just been born and a nightmare's begun.
Ahead of him they'll be no sun.
A little creature's right to life
Is full of only pain and strife.
He needs to see the light of day.
Instead it's trucks and crates to stay.
Shipped across the world in fright
All the day and through the night.
Crying for a mum he's never known.
He's sad deprived and all alone.
He'll never see grass the earth or sky.
The truth he's just been born to die.
Surely he's entitled to a little life
Before he has to face the knife.
We ask how can this really be.
Some people just don't seem to see.
I thought we were a compassionate race.
Come on now friends this is a disgrace.

Christine Charlesworth

A HANDFUL OF HOPE
(For a rescued fox cub)

So small
          You fit snugly into my palm.
Tiny and blind,
          Locked in your twilight space
          Of scarce awareness.
          Already you have learned
Harsh lessons
          Of hunger, cold, abandonment,
          The loss of a warm, dark world.

So weak
>   Curled in my fingers' clasp.
>   Your thread of life
>   Fragile as gossamer;
Yet oddly tenacious
>   As breath succeeds breath
>   And each new hour blossoms with hope
>   That your small frame
Will draw strength
>   From this sheltering hand.
>   That endeavour will be enough
>   To assure you the certainty
Of new tomorrows.

Joan Howes

VEAL? NO DEAL
(Dedicated to Jill Phipps)

I'm stuck in a box and I can't get out
Around me, I hear the screams and shouts.
People protesting to leave me alone
All that's left of me is skin and bone,
The engines running, petrol fumes
I know for sure I won't escape this room.
I hope they'd take pity and let us go
But obviously their answer is no
Why me? Why me? Why take me away
Let me just live for one more day
The people outside risk their lives for mine
Chaining themselves to the lorry - is that a crime?
Fighting for what they believe in.
Tell me, is that a sin?
But I'm still stuck in this cramped cell
Travelling down the road to hell

Becki Potter

159

TRAPPED

Why am I here,
Peering through the bars of my metal cage?
I sense the rumble of the road beneath.
It seems we're on a journey
To a fateful factory,
Where things unmentionable
Are done to chickens.
I have a dream!
I'd like to wander by an open stream
And feel the spring breeze ruffling each feather,
To stand outside in beautiful weather,
To be free!
My life so far has been spent in a shed.
I suppose I might as well be dead.
Could I escape?
If I could only wriggle through these bars
And chance an early flight,
Would I then make it to another world,
A world of perpetual light?
Or would I drop like some great stone
Down on the road, and then experience
An instant crushing by a careless car
Hurrying to its destination?
No! I am trapped,
Doomed to see this journey through
To the bitter end!
A chicken has no friend.

Susan Jarvis

RECIPE FOR LOVE

'Recipe for Love' they call it -
Take one sheep, pig, cow or chicken, preferably young and scared,
intensively rear it, fatten it, bully it,
do what you like to it, it's only an animal, after all.
Kick it on the lorry with all the others, then drag it off the other end.
Grabbing hands usher it closer to death.
Stun it - sometimes - prepare the instruments of murder,
then cut its throat and let it bleed. It's only an animal, after all.
Death brings peace at last.
'Recipe for Love', they call it -
'Recipe for Hate', more like.

'Recipe for Love', they call it -
Cancer, heart disease, chemical poisoning, that's what they won't say.
Muckdonalds, Murder King, Dewhearse -
scavengers, thieves, harbingers of death,
ravage rainforests, plunder countryside,
poison people with tainted flesh.
Take five football pitches, grow soya and feed sixty-one;
rear cattle from the same land, and feed two.
Meanwhile the third world starves. But they're only humans, after all.
'Recipe for Love', they call it -
'Recipe for Death', more like.

Amanda George

6 MONTHS OF LIFE

If only I could shed a
Tear
To show how much I really
Fear

Instead I have to face
The fate
Of being veal upon a
Plate

I wish my life was a little longer
But this will never be
All the while men like Gilder ship us across
The sea.

I've forgotten the way my mum's milk
Tastes
And the way her tongue used to lick my
Face.

I've stood in this crate for 6 months and
Fear my fate has come.
I can hardly walk
I am stiff and sore, I stumble as my knees
Hit the floor.

Rough hands handle me to my feet
They shove me through a door
This is not the doorway to heaven
As I am dragged along the blood-stained floor.

Carly Rosewell (16)

FOR THE DUMB

I could believe the times are evil
And the minds of men are mad,
That the innocent will suffer
And the slaughter never cease.
I could believe our work is fruitless,
That the governments will win,
And the dumb will be forgotten
And their silent pleas unheard.
I could believe that power triumphs,
That the rich hold all the strings,
With their meetings and committees
And their influential friends -
But I don't.

Because love will take us forward,
And love will find a way
To release the bonds that hold them
And let reason have her sway.
Love will make us stronger and
Touch those who still are blind,
Those that need awakening to
The slaughter and the crimes.
And we will find the money and
The strength to fight the fight,
A fight that promotes reason and
Compassion against might -
We have to.

Because they need us, every one of us,
Until the war is won.
They need the ones who read their minds,
The ones who are not dumb.

Rita Bradshaw

NO RIGHT AT ALL

What right have we humans to keep
Caged in a prison,
Any animal or bird or fish belonging
To God's kingdom.

What gives us the right to deny,
Budgies and canaries no room to fly.
If we're locked up it's because
We've usually done wrong,
And not because from our throats
Comes a beautiful song.

Where's the compassion in locking up those
Who love to dig sandy tunnels with their toes;
How many hours in a day are they left alone
In a box we laughably call their home.

Little furry creatures so cute to see -
To stroke and to hold on our knee;
To give as a present to a child who
Soon gets tired and finds other things to do.

What right have we to geld a horse
Or geld any animal of course;
Why should they run until they drop
And 'til they are old it doesn't stop.
Some despise the chasing of a fox;
At least he has a chance to be free and
Not locked up in a box.

What of those who smugly say we shouldn't eat meat,
But by the way, keep guinea pigs and birds in cages
Left to themselves for ages and ages.
We call these little creatures our little pets
But prison for their beauty is what they get.
So what right have we to treat them so badly.
Because they're so small,
We have no right to do it, no right at all.

Mavis Hardy

HUMANITY . . . NOT VIVISECTION

What more could one ask for today
The sun, blue tranquil sea . . .
Wild birds and friendly animals
That come so trustingly . . .
With so much given with Thy Love,
Beauty of trees and flowers . . .
Why then, should hearts become like stone
To mar these happy hours?
One thing, oh Lord, that I would ask,
That You will come again,
To guide the way, for those that stray,
Who cause such grief and pain
Inflicted on dumb animals
To satisfy the mind.
When only man himself can serve
To benefit mankind.
> Release those victims from such traps
> Of agonies untold,
> Who had no voice, and not from choice,
> Were born to die for gold.

D L Rayner-Campbell

OUR FAMILY DOGS 1996

Zoe and Mak a happy pair,
rescued from a life of despair.
Mak mistreated, such a gentle face,
Zoe, lost from her home without trace.
Both needing love away from the chill
now putting their trust in Ross and Gill.
At last happy, well fed, and warm,
nothing to fear and safe from harm.

Out in the Paddock romping around,
Mak, younger than Zoe, knows no bound.
Running like a fox with long legs telling,
Zoe doing her best, aged nine, mellowing.
Giving such joy, content together,
no worries now whatever the weather.

Looking after the house they know is home,
Strangers can fear their bark alone.
Showing their thanks, the best they learn.
Guarding and waiting the family return.
Great excitement, thankful greeting,
Safely returned, a happy meeting.

Never forgetting little Zak.
A kindly soul, before Mak.
Never angry, He seemed to smile.
A pretty dog who stayed a while.
He passed away, to great dismay,
But we will see Him again one day.

Ivy E Baker

THE COLOUR RED

The morning sun no longer shines within these prison walls
Each cell speaks of the misery within
No more the open spaces and the freedom of the wild
Each day one more experiment begins.

How can man ever justify this terrible abuse
These creatures have the right to live their lives
The safe use of cosmetics is a fatuous excuse
The tormented in their pain will not survive.

Vain women flaunt their coats of fur their vanity appeased
The blood that's spilled they do not have a care
When viewed with horror and disdain they never feel displeased
Their arrogance displayed in what they wear.

The red, the black, the stirrup cup, the hounds pick up the scent
The fox and stag are caught and torn to shreds
These degenerate men and women celebrate their cruel event
Their children brought to witness this bloodshed.

Man is not a Demigod with licence to destroy
Society has a debt they must repay
To animals who loyally serve and only ask for love
Who guide and bring us comfort day by day.

Audrey Robbins

UNKIND REGARDS

Cub-hunting in August.
     Earths stopped, cover at dawn:
     yells, slaps - fox cubs torn!
Treat 'meat' humanely!
     Livestock drivers rest and eat.
     Their stifled loads? They're only meat!
Killers for fur-fillers.
     Men show their greed - insanity
     by killing for tarts' vanity.
Profitable atrocities
     Batteries! Ivories! Less tigers roar!
     When greed takes control, then cruelties soar.
Be a show-stopper!
     Bull, cock or dog fights; badger-baiting
     are shows that sadists find elating.
Show some horse sense.
     If riders were killed like the horses,
     they'd abolish those cruel jump-courses.
Horrific deaths.
     Some creatures die with head in a can -
     left thoughtlessly there by litter-lout-man.
Cold-blooded killers.
     Fox hunters etcetera are harassed at will -
     yet unharried rod-fishermen torture and kill!
Tortured calves.
     No daylight, no freedom and cruelty's real,
     so just ponder this as you contemplate veal.
Cruelty grows in ratio to selfishness.
     We're more unkind to animals
     than ever as a nation. (23.3.1992)
     That follows! For our kiddies now get scant consideration.

Tony Hughes-Southwart

RESPECT

Animals roam this land
We are not the only ones
Their life is precious
Just like ours
They should not be made to die.

To be hunted down
Shot at and killed
When they should be roaming free,
To feather nests for humans
It's just wicked, can't they see.

A coat that's on a tiger
It's where it's supposed to be
Not covering some human
So we should let them be.

A seal wallows in a lovely pool,
And sits upon the shore
It's place is there, so leave it,
We don't need it anymore.

All animals have feelings
And were free
Long before we came
So let us have respect for them
And let them live their lives.

We should all learn to live beside them,
It isn't asking much
So go on respect them
They ask nothing more from us.

H Webb

JUST MOLLY!

Look at her! Oh so jolly,
Our kitten, called just Molly.

Four white paws, for shoes,
The litter box, she does use!

Well behaved, full of mischief,
She chews our plant for feed!

A playful, vibrant bundle,
Down the stairs, she can thumble.

She loves to pose as if a naughty child,
Even kittens have an intelligent mind!

We are not sure, if she knows her name,
To her, any noise is the same.

Into the bedroom at night,
She is creeping out of sight!

Around dawn, we hear a big yawn,
We look at each other and frown.

Molly! Beside us, had a good sleep,
Purring, her two big eyes peep!

Yes! This is our tiny, furry bundle,
Out of bed, we too, thumble!

Now, we do not need a clock to wake,
Nor a TV programme is at stake!

Molly, has the first choice,
As soon as she hears our voice.

When we turn the key in the door,
She is there, waiting, evermore.

For our Kitten we do care,
Hope, her life with us she'll share.

Eva Rose

MY DOGGIE DAY

When light of day has just began
Until the last of setting sun
I know how best to pass the day
On Dornoch Links just out to play
First I dive into the burn
Then on and on and on I go
Picking up the odd wee stone
Then I'm off into a bunker
Where I lie and wait on hunkers
Sometimes I find something that smells
Oh how this makes my walker yell
I race along this great big ditch
And claim it as my own true pitch
And who knows if I have some luck
At the other end I'll be covered in muck
It sure is fun to go out and roam
Especially as I am not alone
And after this great glorious run
I rest at home as I am done
When light of day has just begun
I'm up and ready for my next run

Moira Thorburn

THE MISSING LINK

They smoke me out, they rein me in.
They make me fight their wars,
They lock me up to cry behind
The prisons they call doors.

To test their perfumes and their paints,
They make me cough and wheeze,
They fill my lungs with filthy smoke,
And cancerous disease.

They make me travel through the night,
They starve or overfeed,
They take my milk, they fence me in,
They put me on a lead.

They make me beg and shake a tin,
They eat me for their luncheon,
They steal my young, or even worse,
They club them with a truncheon.

They muzzle me, they doctor me,
They dig me with their spur,
They blind my eye, they cut me up,
They sell my tusks and fur.

They track me down and slaughter me,
A death so mean and slow,
They make me fight against my own,
While shouting 'Tally-ho!'

Oh God who made both man and beast,
They need to learn anew,
That when they raise their hand to me,
They raise their hand to you!

Peter Davies

DOLPHINS

Creatures of the ocean, wild and free,
Surviving the world in harmony.
Swimming together in unison and faith,
They bring such joy to the human race.

Spinning and turning, splashing their fun,
They bring a peace to everyone.
Living life to the full in their ocean playground,
Keeping in touch with their language of sound.

The sea is theirs, to do as they please,
Relaxed and happy, inhaling the breeze.
Shadow of a boat, they swim nearer to see,
Only to be caught and no longer be free.

Now in a pool, thirty feet across,
They swim dreaming of the ocean they lost.
Friends and family left behind,
All they see are faces - so kind!

Made to do tricks, to entertain us,
They give the little they have, and that is love.
Go close to them and look in their eyes,
You will see that soon they'll die.

Only when we've gone to our families at home,
Does the sad eyed dolphin quietly roam.
Restlessly swimming around and around,
Yearning for the ocean sound.

Death at last does set them free,
And back in their playground they will be.
Home once more to turn and spin,
Re-united with their kin.

Julie McLennan

THE PUPPY'S TALE

I trotted sadly down the road and looked from left to right,
But no-one even noticed me or recognised my plight.
I was alone in deep despair without the warmth of home,
My owners did not really care and turned me out to roam.
I had to search for scraps of food, from everybody's bins,
And people quickly chased me off or kicked me on my shins.
I think I was a Christmas gift or something of the sort,
They seemed to love me at the time, at least that's what I thought.
I wandered round for days and days,
In search of food and love.
But no-one gave me anything,
Except a spiteful shove.
A lady spied me in the rain and stroked my weary head.
'You poor neglected little thing'
I think is what she said.
She took me home and gave me food
A lead and collar too
So now at last I'm fed and warm,
My tale is all too true.

Juliet C Eaton

EXPERIMENTAL POEM

When you're puffing your Embassy Regal,
You can be sure they're tested by beagles.
Enjoy your mascara, another bad habit,
But spare a thought for the eyes of a rabbit.
Scents and perfumes might smell nice,
But what about disfigured mice?
Vaccine and pills your symptons ease,
I bet the monkey disagrees.

So I think before you buy and pay,
For some poor creature has had its day.
All in all without a doubt,
It's a pity beasts can't shout.
Would you care? I bet you can,
But it is not the plight of man.
Something now is sadly lacking,
Animal testers! Send them packing.

Emma Weber (12)

/

LAST STAND

Crack, a bullet wings its deadly way into the sky,
to the earth a creature falls in bloody agony to die,
The hunter is victorious as he moves among the trees,
anything in his sights will never again live or breathe.
Shot shatters bone, an animal lies dying in its own gore,
its eyes are panicstricken, to die like this what is it all for?
He's a brave man isn't he? He has nerves to face the beast,
but he doesn't mention that creature is defenceless to say the least!
Oh yes, he's a brave man alright, completely without fear,
as he blasts away at a pregnant shy roe deer.
He's only happy when surrounded by pierced fur and broken feather,
bodies scattered around, death throes among the heather.
When the carnage is over the last creature will stand its ground and speak out,
'Are you satisfied, are you now done? Your world is finished, of that there is
no doubt.
We were a thing of beauty, we were a creation of wonder,
Killing us will remain man's biggest ever blunder.'

Brian Land

TINY

Tiny was our last and most beloved cat;
She was fifteen years old when she died,
And her passing broke our hearts.
Whenever we want a picture of love,
We think of Tiny, and there see love.
She never strayed beyond the home -
She was always present,
Amidst every joy and sorrow.
She was tiny in size, and grey in colour,
And she had a heart of gold;
A heart of affection and understanding,
Of kindness and tenderness and loyalty.
Tiny, we miss you so much,
That no-one can replace you!
Thank you for what you were and gave -
May we meet again some happy day!

David Houston

MY TWO BEST FRIENDS

I have two cats
That mean the world to me
They have been with me
Since I was three
They are always there
When I need them
They always seem to listen
When I have a problem
They always make me laugh
With their silly little ways
They show me their love
By the way they act
My world wouldn't be the same
Without my two best friends.

Sarah Marshall

ANIMAL RIGHTS

All done up in her finery
Preening like a bird
Coat of arms outstanding
Selected from the herd
Does it make her feel beautiful
Adorned in another's skin?
Does she feel more intelligent
Sporting fur of my next of kin?
Her fashion coat won't last her
'Twill end up at car boot
The life taken so needlessly
Now merely a point mute
Humans are a species
We don't care much about
We try hard to evade them
Nature's law we do not flout
They think they are preserving
This green 'was' pleasant land
But with respect we'll tell you
Their heads are in the sand
We know our place in nature
Have respect for our domain
We save our skins whene'er we can
If only humans would refrain . . .

Margarette L Damsell

BRING ME THE BEAST WITH A WIZARD'S FOOT

On a cold bleak winter's night mankind slept
Beneath the warmth of his kingdom.
Hardly stirring as thoughts chased their never ending tails.
This was true but for one man; who
Dreamt he was a hunter.
Freedom allowed his mind to wander unshackled
Across the emerald carpet of nature's domain.
Such was his feeling of pleasure
That at one time he knew:
He knew he'd caught a glimpse of heaven.
Whilst upon these travels he came across the sight of brother mink
Sleeping soundly amongst his loving family
And safe beneath the cloak of darkness.
The hunter smiled for such was this marvel; that
He stood quietly bewitched.
With stomach full, his thoughts were not of the kill
But to take pleasure in something wondrous.
Such was his feeling of awe.
That at one time he knew:
He knew he'd caught a glimpse of beauty.
Suddenly, without warning or reason, the dream changed
With startled eyes and rigid bone, fear oozed from his brother's skin
Too scared to run, the heavy hand of mankind
Sank deep into the head of innocence
And as the blackness reached into the very soul
A sound of churlish laughter was heard
Ringing freely into blood-soaked ears.
Such was his feeling of terror
That at one time he knew:
He knew he'd caught a glimpse of hell.

G B Holland

AGNUS DEI

What place in the Divine Plan
those the God within forgets, and the devil in man recall;
the battery hen, the caged bird, the veal calf,
and the lamb,
the lamb of God.
No wonder that in church we ask
that mercy be shown to us the merciless.
How strange the state of vivisectionist's soul
performing needless torture in a so-called enlightened age.
Heartless deeds committed in, the name of humanity.
Never are we less than animals - who cleanly kill
or not at all - than when at our evil task, bringing
relief to men at cost of fear and pain.
Is 'Heaven in a rage,' at the massacres, atrocities so large
they are never found in nature's world, nor
the ignorance that twists beauty into beastliness
behind closed laboratory doors, or gluttony that
takes the flesh that lived, looked to the sun,
on meadow, by flowing brook, not just for survival's sake;
or those creatures that knew a brief and cruel span
but long in anguish and fear
only the short dark senseless misery of despair
the cage, the cell, then stench of death the living Hell,
- the abattoir;
the poor imprisoned hen, plucked raw, terror in the gentle
bovine eyes in the frightening sickening wait for
the blank-eyed, dull -witted assassin's bloodied hand;
The words of the Agnus Dei, rising in the air, that this sin be taken
away - cries in the night, men cannot, and will not hear:

Allyson Kennedy Kiddle

ODE TO AMADEUS (THE HORSE)

Across the meadows
Through the trees
A willow weeps
In the Zephyr's heave

The moon shines high
And stars to guide
The world seems lost
With time to bide

Then through the forest
Bathed in light
He strides with pride
And noble might

The ebony coat
Those gleaming eyes
Only his vigour
Stills the swallow's cries

His charismatic power
Expels such a force
That none can deter
This master from his course

Onwards he paces
As the lesser bow their heads
For they have not the courage
To follow where he treads.

Dawn-Marie Gibbons

THROUGH THE EYES OF A DOG

Here they come the menaces,
I wish they'd live at school,
I suppose I'd better greet them,
Or they'll take me for a fool.

I don't care if they throw the stick,
They can get it themselves today,
It's too cold now the winter's here,
In the garden I'll not play.

Now where's my bone gone,
I'll put it in the ground,
And chew it at my leisure,
When the menaces are not around.

I'll lick his hand, climb on his lap,
And pray that he don't find,
His slipper I enjoyed today,
With the hole in right behind.

Still pets they are and pets they'll stay,
While they work and feed me good,
I'll give them all a run later,
And chase them through the wood.

Now tea-time is all over,
My tummy is full,
I'll shut my eyes, no wood for me,
No, I am not a fool.

Kathleen Brice

BUT THEY FEEL, AND THEY BLEED

He came to say goodbye -
My train was about to leave.
He kissed me sweetly on the cheek,
And gave me a . . . shoebox -
It surprised me. Shyly he said
'For you.' Klaus - I remember,
His name was Klaus.

The train left the station.
Intrigued I opened the box - its lid
Was full of holes.
I discovered a small guinea-pig - how lovely!
Tiny eyes looked up at me, as if to say
'Hello'. I saw words
In the shoebox. On one side

Klaus had written ' My name is Desiree,
I hope you will love me, as my master
Loves you.'
I did love Desiree. Looked after my new friend
As best I could. Klaus was now far away.
Teenage crush . . . Miles separated us.
I did love Desiree. Treasured a memory . . .

One day I came back from school -
Desiree was missing. Horrified
I was told
That my brother had taken the small guinea-pig,
That he had given it to his science teacher.
It was just one of those things . . .
They needed 'something' to dissect.

Claire-Lyse Sylvester

RESPECT AND PROTECT

Consider a mink, stealing your clothes,
To fashion a hat for its head.
Give thought to a seal, trying to steal
Your skin, before you were dead.

If a crocodile, with an evil smile,
Had you made into bags and shoes;
Or you warmed the neck of a wily fox.
You'd perhaps feel rather abused.

A bear or a tiger scraping you clean,
With a look quite priggish and smug,
Could leave you feeling insulted,
As you lay on their floor as a rug.

You would certainly feel quite indignant,
Or something akin to a fool,
If a rhino cruelly ended your days,
Then mounted your head on its wall.

So, why do we interfere with their world?
What on earth can we possibly gain?
Why don't we respect them as kindred souls,
Instead of causing such pain?

Bernard Curtis

FOX HUNTING

Across the morning air,
Across the fields of dew,
A sound disturbs the silent dawn,
Alieu, Alieu, Alieu.

Where Renard rests from work well done,
In a far off leafy dell,
Comes a sound that stops his heart,
It is the huntsman's yell.

Other sounds he's heard before,
He heard once more this day,
The sound of horn and baiting hounds,
Tis time to be away.

Over hills through gorse and bush,
Through streams and fields of hay.
With pounding heart and aching legs,
He flees the miles away.

Pausing in some leafy lane,
He knows the race is won,
It was not for him the hounds did cry,
Some other fox had gone . . .

G h Hall

STOP

Stop!
I've seen it before,
A hand comes down and takes a friend,
Can't stand it anymore.

Don't!
The sight hurts too much
To see friends of mine reduced to
A state of blood and guts.

Wait!
I don't understand
What have we done to deserve this?
It's getting out of hand

Who
Gave you the right
To rule our lives and rule our deaths,
To rule our days and nights?

Hope
Acts as our keeper
You act like someone made you God
But, you're just the grim reapers.

Jennifer Emey

UNIVERSAL PRAYER

I am a falcon, flying high and free,
Inhaling pollutants from fume and factory.
My feathers clogged and colourless,
Oh please stop before you destroy all of us.

I am a fox, roaming woodland glade,
trying to feed my cubs but such mess man has made.
Strewing plastic bags, tin cans all around,
burying the beauty, driving us underground.

I am a dolphin swimming in sea so blue,
It looks perfect but chemicals ships bestrew,
Killing my brothers and sisters, food contaminating,
Undoing all the good that God did creating.

I am the mink pursued for my rich lustrous fur,
To adorn the vanity of people, supply allure,
Unfeeling of my pain and suffering,
Their eyes unseeing and ears unhearing.

Please stop before you destroy us all,
Save this wonderful world, catch before we fall.
We cannot turn the clock back, we can slow it down,
If we all pull together, we are all here on Earth,
To preserve it for posterity and total re-birth.

Patricia Jane Webb

POOR FOXY

As I roamed o'er hill and dale,
A fox flashed past my side,
Then twenty hounds with men in red,
'Tally ho!' They cried.

I watched them slowly gaining,
They caught him by the brook,
With whips and sticks they beat him,
It sickened me to look.

One grabbed him by the tail,
And fumbled in his coat,
Amid the cheers he took a knife,
And cut poor Foxy's throat.

Next I saw the awful sight,
A nature lover dreads,
He threw poor Foxy to the pack,
I watched him torn to shreds.

Tonight you'll see them drink a toast,
Pathetic men in red,
How proud and brave those fiends will feel,
As Foxy lies there dead.

John Napier Williams

TOMMY

His eyes are a curious yellow
His gait is a regal one,
In his barred, orange coat,
Designer please note,
He slinks along in the sun.
No tradesman's entrance for him,
It's the front door or nothing it seems,
His Zebras are mice, his gazelles are birds,
His body's a she-cat's dream.
His roar's a delicious purr,
Pride breaths through every pore,
Where survival is hard, in suburban backyard
He keeps his well-filled store.
Though a cat, at heart he's a lion,
Dreaming lion-sized dreams on the mat,
A marmalade renegade, who parades in the shade,
And kills flies in ten seconds flat.

Georgina Cook

SOPHISTICAT

A perfect feline figure,
A picture of elegance,
Almighty ruler of her sophisticated empire.

The empress hypnotises all,
With her smooth grey coat, her piercing blue stare,
Dangerous, mystical beauty.

Stretched proudly across her ice blue silk sheets,
Surrounded by velvet cushions,
She sniffs superiorly at her smoked salmon breakfast.

The slave will leave to the unknown outside world soon,
Leaving the feline to prowl her luxurious territory,
And think her majestic thoughts.

So secretive and mysterious,
Refined in every way,
But deep down, her wild heart cries out.

Kathryn Hughes

INFORMATION

We hope you have enjoyed reading this book - and that you will continue to enjoy it in the coming years.

If you like reading and writing poetry drop us a line, or give us a call, and we'll send you a free information pack.

Write to

Poetry Now Information
1-2 Wainman Road
Woodston
Peterborough
PE2 7BU